Musings of
Kev the Kiwi

Ponder some of life's biggest questions
with an eccentric electrician.

Kevin Missen

Written by Kevin Missen
Published by Missen Publishing
E: missen.k@xtra.co.nz
© 2019 Kevin Missen

This is a work of non-fiction.

This book is copyright. Except for the purpose of fair review, no part may be stored or transmitted in any form or by any means, electronic or mechanical, including recording or storage in any information retrieval system, without permission in writing from the publishers. No reproduction may be made, whether by photocopying or by any other means, unless a licence has been obtained from the publisher.

Cataloguing in Publication Data:
Title: Musings of Kev the Kiwi
ISBN: 978-0-473-47073-9 (pbk.)
ISBN: 978-0-473-47074-6 (epub) Subjects: New Zealand Non-Fiction, Memoir, Autobiography

Cover design and page layout by
Janet Curle, wildsidedesign.net

First printing 2019 yourbooks.co.nz
International distribution Ingram Spark 2019

Contents

	Introduction	5
1	In the Beginning	7
2	Black Dog; My Mother's Story	9
3	Early Days	13
4	Rampage on the Rocks	18
5	Mowing Lawns	23
6	Perpetual-motion and energy generation	26
7	School	30
8	Depression	34
9	Te Reo Maori	36
10	Mischief Years	37
11	Parihaka	39
12	Bikes	41
13	Trains	44
14	Cars	48
15	Smoking	61
16	Politics	62
17	The Media	68
18	Our Historical Building	69
19	The Complaint	71
20	The Interview	74
21	Letter to the Editor	77

22	The Knife	78
23	Modern Technology	81
24	Old Age	83
25	Where Am I?	84
26	The Horticultural Group	86
27	Work Stories	87
28	Flies	95
29	Cups and Saucers	96
30	The Root of all Evil	97
31	Hatred and Unforgiveness	99
32	Sorry!	101
33	The Justice System	102
34	The Welfare System	105
35	Christmas	108
36	The Gift	110
37	Time Travel	111
38	The Meaning of Life	113
39	The God Connection	115
40	A Brief Description of What I Believe	126
41	What Next?	129
42	The Word Trip	130
	Other Books by Kevin Missen	132

Introduction

I used to think that truth was an absolute. Something either happened a particular way, or it didn't. Someone's description of an event was either right, or wrong. I now know different! Two different people can describe the same thing differently; both believing they are telling the absolute truth. If either one of them changed their minds, they would be telling a lie.

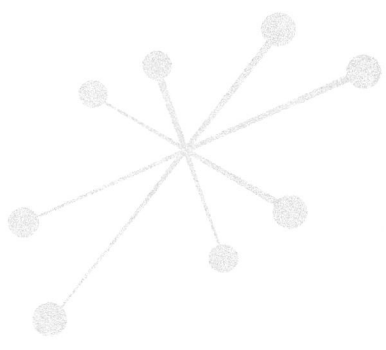

We all see and understand things differently, from our own perspective. Even concepts of right and wrong are taught to us differently. We need to understand this before we judge or criticise others.

This story is mine. I love writing. I write fact and fiction, poetry and prose, songs and sermons, ditties and dirges; anything that comes into my head. This book is a combination of most of the above. I'm not telling lies, but I do invoke my poetic licence from time to time, to embellish an otherwise mundane event. I am writing this because it gives me pleasure to do so, and I believe that there are snippets of wisdom and pleasure that I can pass on to others.

You are not allowed to agree with everything I say, otherwise it will be plagiarism of my ideas!

I call all my writings 'living documents' so I have the right to (and probably will) tweak and change things at each printing. You may be reading a limited edition copy! Feedback is always welcome, but most of all, I hope you enjoy reading this as much as I enjoyed writing it!

One

In the Beginning

My grandmother's house was very old. It was the 1960s and she still had the old vented safe in the wall and three big pull out bins that were hinged at the bottom and held bulk flour, sugar, and grain for the chickens. The spare bed that I used to have my afternoon sleeps in, pulled down out of the wall with a counterweight spring mechanism.

The only toilet was outside; about 10 meters from the back door, via an uneven cobblestone path, in an un-lined and un-lit corrugated iron shed that was covered by a large passionfruit vine. The cistern was high up on the back wall to gravity-feed down and was operated by a long chain, hanging down the left hand side. Grandad had put a rope extension on it with a wooden handle; so we kids could reach.

In big letters on the toilet bowl were the words, 'Vitreous China'. Me, being a young boy with limited reading skills, read it as 'victorious' China. There were only two meanings for the word China that I knew of; one was the country, China and the other was used to describe the objects in the old china cabinet. I don't recall ever seeing a toilet bowl in anyone's china cabinet, so I assumed that the bowl was made in China; but more than that, was made in 'victorious' China.

The little I knew about the country, China, was that it had a lot of people and a big army. I assumed that they had a great battle victory, and what better way to advertise it, than to stamp it on toilet bowls where it would be seen by every person in the world?

Grandma met Granddad on the ship, while both were immigrating to New Zealand in the 1920s. He was German, and was travelling with his son, Sidney, to work at the Porirua Lunatic Asylum, as it was then known; apparently to instigate or develop electric shock treatment.

Grandma thought she was marrying a rich psychiatric doctor and that they would travel the world together. The truth was that they lived on site with the patients and she was very unhappy!

Two

Black Dog; My Mother's story
(written by Vera Missen, several years ago)

Cancer took my sister's life three months ago, aged 82. Her last words to me were, "I have had a hard life, but a good one." As I said my final farewell by the side of her open coffin, I noticed the wrinkles of age and worry had been smoothed away. Only a faint scar on her neck was visible.

Hilda left behind a legacy few know; about a now tatty, dusty, rotting black velvet dog, which still stirs memories of an unnamed psychiatric patient who had designed it.

In the 1920s, our parents rented a house in the grounds of Porirua Mental Asylum, as it was then known. This was a hospital which hid its villas from public view and, to which visitors came furtively and infrequently, with a sense of shame that their loved ones should be 'put away'.

When Hilda was a small child, she became seriously ill and a breathing tube needed to be inserted to save her life. She would not have survived the long trip into Wellington Hospital, so our father carried her across the driveway into the arms of a skilled doctor, who immediately operated. Hilda was placed in isolation and the doctor was unable to give our anxious parents a reassuring prognosis. Convalescence was slow.

An old man, who we called Granddad Vaughan, believed in the power of prayer. My parents knew he was praying, when one afternoon, a patient shuffled into the room escorted by an orderly, who asked Mother's permission to allow this man to visit. He stood by Hilda's bed, stroked her arm and grunted things mother couldn't understand. Immediately, a miracle happened! Instead of fear, Hilda's eyes lit up and there emerged an almost magnetic connection between the two. Neither could speak, but both would communicate through smiles and garble.

The next afternoon, he came and placed in Hilda's arms, a velvet dog. Black Dog had long floppy ears, a thick knotted tail, and the kindest button eyes a spaniel ever had. This was the turning point in Hilda's recovery.

Black Dog got handed around and ended up in the arms of my young son, Kevin. Broken hearts have dripped tears, soaking his coat; many secrets have entered his ears; and he has enthroned chairs, prams, carts and bikes. There was panic when he got lost in a hospital but elation when a bus driver returned him after being lost for many days. Children and adults became thoughtful as they listened to the story of a man; hidden away in an institution, forgotten by family and friends; who had such a loving heart he fashioned a soft toy for a small child.

Sometime later we moved to Johnsonville and we had no further contact with acquaintances we knew. Black Dog has lost his tail, those long floppy ears have long gone, and his insides spill out of his worn body. Did Hilda survive because of Grandad Vaughan's prayers? Did those secret groanings from a retarded man, bring her new life? May it have been the comfort from a black velvet dog? Only God knows. Today, Black Dog is resting in an old suitcase; too old to be handled, but too precious for the scrap heap.

Black Dog
by Me

I have a Black Dog
Black Dog is his name.
He is old and scruffy
But I love him just the same.

I brush his fur and pat his head
And talk to him all night long.
Somehow he seems to understand
When anything is wrong.

I never give him Dog food
He shares my food with me.
He has Weetbix for his breakfast
And potato with his tea!

At night he comes to bed with me
And we talk about the day,
I tell him that I love him
And he will never go away.

I used to think if I prayed real hard
I'd wake up in the morn
To find Black dog had come alive
And running 'round the lawn.

Others have their Bunny, Bear
Or other favourite toy,
But Black Dog has been my best friend
Since I was a little boy.

Black Dog, repaired

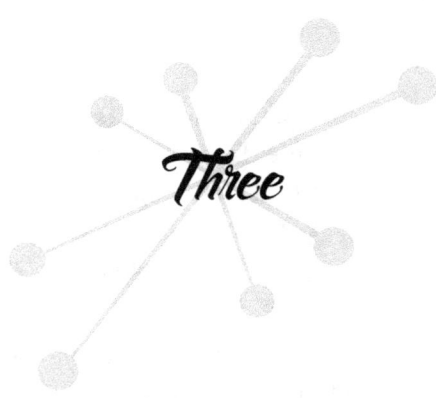

Three

Early days

Mum was very close to her father and half-brother, but her dad died tragically when she was young. Her half-brother, Sidney married and left home, but his new wife left him. He went to look for her and he was never heard from again. Her mother remarried Mr Pearson, a lift engineer, and seemed to have found some happiness.

He let me play in his shed and I would spend hours looking at every object in every drawer and cupboard. The hanging scales were probably the favourite; and my sister, Irene and I would try and guess what everything weighed.

I don't recall anything new in Grandma's house. Even the dinner sets, that I now know are valuable, were in everyday use and the replica-Queen's china carriage and horses were played with like dinky toys.

Christmas lunch, with combined families, was held there for many years; including the traditional Christmas cake, with a penny hidden somewhere in the middle.

Grandma would tell us an old English rhyme:

'Had a little donkey, kept it in the yard,
One day in the winter, when it was snowing hard,
Put it in the parlour so it wouldn't catch a chill,
Bang, bang, bang, it kicked the chandelier,
Took it for a cabbage leaf and bit my mother's ear!'

We had no car, but I had a metal tricycle, with a big tray at the back. Before I turned five, Mum would take me when she did her shopping once a week and the tray would get filled with meat and produce. I don't know if there were many flat roads in Titahi Bay; just various gradients that made journeys difficult or dangerous, depending on whether I was going up or down.

Sometimes Mum would have to push me, or I would have to get off and push. Taking my feet off the pedals, while going downhill was the most dangerous, as the trike would soon build up speed and it was difficult to get my feet back onto spinning pedals! The advantage of this terrain was that trikes, bikes, toys and trolleys could get up to exciting speeds if desired!

One Christmas; I must have been about three years old, my parents got me a metal 'Tonka' transporter truck. It was the perfect size for me to sit on and race down the hill! Other presents were placed inside, but I just tipped them out and headed for the door to try my truck out! It was very frustrating that I had to wait; open the other presents and be sociable before the test drive!

Dad built us a trolley a year or so later. It had the wire-spoked rubber pram wheels that were prevalent at the time. The front axle was attached to a board that had a half inch bolt through the middle, as a steering pivot. This was turned by our feet on the board and the rope; looped between the outer edges by the wheels.

Other kids had similar trolleys, so we could race. I tried one of these other trolleys, but my feet wouldn't reach the board, so I relied on the rope for steering. I got the speed wobbles and stopped by crashing into the neighbour's letterbox! This not only broke the letterbox, but also the two full bottles of milk inside! I had to clean up the mess and do chores, to pay off the milk.

My introduction to burning rubber was when mum bought me some new brakes. She called them Gumboots. I would race down the hill at break-neck speed, and then push my heels hard into the footpath to slow down. This not only left a nice rubber burning smell, but I was proud of the black rubber strip I had left! Sadly, the rubber was not up to racing standard and the heel began quickly disappearing. I can remember having difficulty getting the screws in to reinforce this weak point, but got very excited, when I realised I could make sparks as well as leaving rubber!

We had no T.V. until I was about ten. We had friends up the road that did though, and when important things happened; like the moon-landing or the Wahine Disaster; we would congregate around their black and white T.V. and discuss the latest events. The radio was important and we would listen to serial programmes; like the 'War of the Worlds', 'The Goon Show' radio programme, and children's stories.

Mum used to play the piano, which I always enjoyed, but after six months of piano lessons; realised I had no natural talent to play myself. Mum never liked the T.V. and reckoned it stopped her playing the piano.

I loved climbing trees! We had very big Macrocarpa trees lining our property and I would climb to the very top, even on windy days, and day dream. I could see for miles and nobody could see me. Even if they could, they couldn't get to me. If war ever broke out and an invading army attacked, I was going to hide up the tree with a sniper rifle. I made sure that I had a stash of important things hidden in the tree, just in case!

It was good training for me for later, when I was a power-board electrician contracted to Transpower, as I have no fear of heights or movement. I would later service the aircraft lights at the top of the Radio Rhema transmission mast at Mahia; 100 metres high and no ladder to climb up. I would tuck my safety harness into my overalls so it wouldn't catch on anything, and climb up the structure. At the top, I would climb out and hook myself on to change the light bulbs.

The 2YA National Programme radio-mast was on the hill close to our house. It was 220 metres high, the second tallest structure in New Zealand at the time. I saw some guys climbing part way up, when I was about 13 years old, and rushed up to the base and asked if I could climb it too. They obviously had to say no, but they were very friendly and showed me through the control room.

The part that fascinated me most was that the fluorescent lights would not turn off. They took a spare tube out of the cupboard and carried it outside. The tube glowed while they held it in their hand, without any electrical connection. They explained how the electromagnetic radiation was strong enough to power the light. This was partly the reasoning for me wanting to be an electrician.

The mast was on a hill surrounded by farmland that dropped off to steep cliffs above the rocky, west-coast shoreline. It's no wonder I was not interested in T.V. when we did get it, as nothing could compete with wandering over farm land; watching animals being born; rescuing animals and birds that fell out of nests; catching tadpoles and watching them change into frogs; climbing up steep cliff faces with bare hands and feet; exploring natural caves and holes; finding geckos under rocks and baby rabbits in rabbit holes; sliding down steep grassy slopes on bits of cardboard and finding the biggest crabs we could!

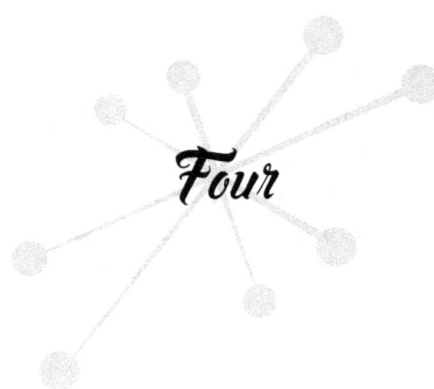

Four

Rampage on the Rocks

We were very fortunate in being brought up in the little suburb of Titahi Bay. Wellington City was about 20 miles (32 km) away. Porirua Harbour, with its launches, yachts, occasional sea plane and the much anticipated annual speedboat regatta was only 3 miles away. The farm lands and hills around Mount Cooper were walked and explored many times and the beach was only 10 minutes' walk from our home. But the greatest excitement of all was to be gained from the rocks. They extended in both directions, from the beach northward, right around to the Porirua inlet and southward, too far to know. It gave a boy much esteem in the sight of his peers if he could tackle the boat house rocks, as they were known, and make it to the end without having to turn back.

I was the supreme champion of these rocks, or so I thought, and I knew all the forts, caves and holes throughout the jutting pinnacles and the best stagnant tadpole ponds. I even tackled the rocks at high tide, so I felt it my duty to explore the reaches of the rocky shore in the other direction toward Wellington; even past the sewer outlet that was the usual turning point for a day's exploration.

I had to take a couple of companions along so they could back up my Monday morning brag when I got back to school. David was my first choice because he was my best mate and I considered him 'second only' to myself. My other choice was Jug. I never did remember his real name. Jug wasn't the sort of bloke we would normally have chosen, as he wasn't as hardened as ourselves, but his old man had this long knife; supposedly from Japan during the war, and he could get hold of it for the day. We thought this might be an invaluable piece of equipment to add to our weaponry of much-treasured pocket knives, a sheath knife, two slingshots and packets of Tom Thumbs and Double Happys firecrackers saved over from the last Guy Fawkes'.

We met on the Friday after school at David's place to look at the tides in the newspaper and prepare a list of provisions. Looking at the tides wasn't going to make any difference to our plans but David's mum said you should always look at the tides before going near the sea.

Our check list consisted of matches, some newspaper to start a fire, a length of rope, and the knives (of course), some Band-Aids, chewing gum, and whatever food and drink our mums prepared for us. Jerseys and raincoats were essential this trip, as chances of showers were high, but nothing short of a hurricane would stop us! That night was spent dreaming of great sea monsters, rock slides and enemies we had to fight!

Our rendezvous the next morning was at 8am at the old cannon overlooking the beach. We each arrived bursting with excitement; Jug, with his father's sword hanging from his belt and a story of how he got it from the shed that night.

We half-ran the distance to the sewer outlet; it wasn't very difficult and was "old ground". The outlet pipe was our first check point. We spat out our chewing gum and broke into our lunches to find what sort of biscuits had been packed. They were shared around and devoured in minutes.

"Right, follow me," I said. "We've got to keep moving!"

The next two hours passed very quickly. There were numerous bottles washed up on the shore and each one had to be 'bombed'; while either floating in the water as an enemy boat, or on a rock as an enemy commando. David was the undisputed stone thrower champion, so he eventually had to stand further back. This meant that Jug and I could score some direct hits.

We were tiring a little after all our displays of skills and energy, and David suggested we stop for a rest, for Jug's sake. Much to our disgust, Jug appeared less tired than any of us; which we decided was due to his lighter pack. I wanted to rest too, but since I was leader, I felt it was my decision when and where we should stop; so I decided that this place was 'no good' and we should carry on to the next bay.

None of us wanted to gather much firewood for the fire, but we gathered a pile of nearby driftwood and put it in one big heap. David put the paper under it and set it alight. It caught surprisingly easily and we could see our pile was not going to last long. A stack of seaweed went on top which made loud bangs and a lot of smoke, much to our delight!

Jug found an old aerosol can and threw it on. We stood nearby expectantly to see what would happen and it exploded suddenly, throwing bits of burning wood several metres. Fortunately, apart from a small hole in David's jersey, the only casualty was my hat that got burnt almost in half (I wasn't wearing it at the time).

The others thought this very funny; putting the remains on my head and making silly comments, but I was a bit upset about the loss. I had had it a long time and it always went with me on my expeditions. The fire was put out soon after; when we threw cups of drink and sea water on it to make it steam and sizzle. The barbeque sausages were eaten cold, partly pre-cooked.

Our decision to head home resulted from dark clouds blocking the sun and a cool sea breeze. The journey back always seems longer, even without the fun and frolicking. It wasn't a difficult walk, with a few rocky parts to climb over, but most of the time was spent tramping across loose shingle that tired the calf muscles. The tide had come in, meaning that we had to make some decisions; whether to get wet wading through water or to climb up cliff faces. We chose the climbing every time.

About half way home our excitement was aroused when I spotted a blue penguin. They weren't uncommon around the area, but many appeared to get sick and die around the sewerage outlet area. This one was alive but appeared very sick. We had no bread, or sandwiches left, and it wouldn't have enjoyed chewing gum; so we decided that it was our duty to carry him home.

We named him Percy, which seemed a logical name for a penguin. He was quite heavy and he had to be carried between two of us. He died about 20 minutes later but I still wanted to take him home, get him stuffed, and take him to school. The rain had set in by this time. We were all wet and cold and wondering how much further we had to go. It wasn't long before we realised that we would have to leave the penguin behind, so I hid it behind a bush, intending to return for it later.

Soon the sewer came into sight and our pace increased into a half-run with the thought of warm, dry clothes and a hot meal driving us on. We split up at the old cannon and I tried to run the rest of the way home but my legs wouldn't let me. I walked into the house with a great sense of triumph and tried to tell my family everything at once.

When Monday came I had recovered sufficiently to re-live the story in much exaggerated form to many other wide-eyed, open-mouthed kids, who crowded around to hear and admire the 'undisputed' Rock Explorer Champion!

Five

Mowing lawns

I didn't mind mowing lawns for pocket money. It's satisfying seeing the before and after, and even as a 14 year old, I enjoyed having control over a noisy motor! I wasn't keen on any more work but Mum had organised a visit for me on Saturday morning, and she said that I could always say 'no'.

It was a council flat with a small sloping lawn at the front and a longer flat area at the back. Both lawns were broken by small flower gardens and shrubs. There was an old rusty hand mower with a canvas catcher by the gate; that was a bit of a worry!

I knocked on the door several times before it was opened.

"You must knock loudly," he said. "We don't hear as well as we used to."

I stepped back a bit, not knowing what to say. This man looked like he was 100 years old!

"What's your name?" he asked.

"Kevin," I answered.

"I'm Jack, and will you be mowing my lawns for me?" he continued.

"Yes," I replied.

"Well, we had better get started then hadn't we?"

I wanted to say, "No, I can't use push mowers," but I couldn't.

I didn't want to do them right then either, but couldn't argue with an old man.

The old mower had been oiled where it counted and cut surprisingly well. Jack had a strict procedure regarding which part to mow first, where to empty the catcher, and which flowers to be careful of. He showed me all his flowers and shrubs, explaining how he looked after them. When Jack went back inside, I thought I could quickly finish the rest and get back home, but he was soon back out with a drink and biscuits.

"Sit down on the steps," he said.

It was another half hour before he had finished talking and asking questions, but the stories he told about his childhood were surprisingly interesting.

This routine continued for almost a year. Time meant nothing to Jack and he wanted me to call in every fortnight, regardless whether the lawns needed mowing or not. I was a little sad when I was no longer required to mow his lawns, but I was pleased I had brought some happiness to the last few months of an old man's life.

I could earn $30 on a Saturday morning mowing lawns; which was good money in those days. Other times I simply went door-to-door, asking people if they wanted jobs done. There was always something; from stacking firewood, weeding gardens or cleaning windows, to simply changing a light bulb. It was up to the person to decide what the job was worth. Most people were quite generous.

Dad was manager of Millers Menswear shop by the Sugar Shovel Fountain in the Cuba Mall. I would help in the shop on Friday nights; selling small things like hankies, ties and belts. I bought my 5-speed bike, a radiogram, a silver watch strap, LP records, and later, my Honda 50 from my earnings.

Dad was made redundant in 1975, and moved to Gisborne with Mum and my brother, Phil, in 1976. I had just started my electrical apprenticeship with the Municipal Energy Department, but got my apprenticeship transferred to the Poverty Bay Electric Power Board and moved up in 1977.

I hated the place! Too hot, too many bugs, no tenpin bowling, no roller skating! What do you do in Gisborne? At the time the power board covered 8500 square-kilometres, and we could easily do 7 hours driving, 3 hours work, and get paid overtime! I enjoyed the work and travel.

Before long, I had joined the Gisborne Camera Club, the Gisborne Writers' Group, the Gisborne Country Music Club, and got involved in speedway. After three years, I had decided that Gisborne was paradise, and was never going to leave!

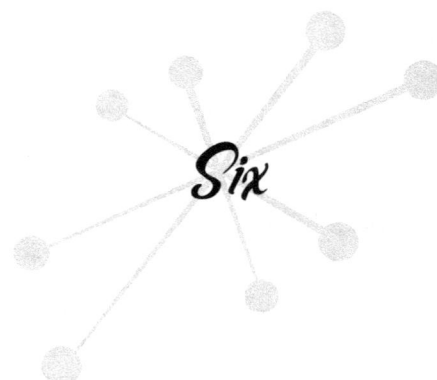

Six

Perpetual-Motion and Energy Generation

This may well be the most important chapter, for the right person. It has the potential to turn somebody into a multi-millionaire!

I have been working on a perpetual-motion machine for about 30 years, on-and-off, and built two prototypes. They didn't work, but they weren't designed to. They proved that my theory was sound. I just haven't seemed to find the time and resources to follow through these days; so I am happy to share some of what I've learned, for others to work on. I know more than what I am revealing here, and am quite happy to work with another, to achieve a positive outcome. I know that you can't go against the laws of nature, but I truly believe that there is either an untapped energy source, or an unutilised, known energy source. I believe this involves either, water or magnetism; possibly both.

There have always been rumours of people that have invented perpetual-motion machines, or vehicles that run on water. They are usually purported to have just disappeared, or to have gone strangely silent; due to either being paid off to be quiet, or having themselves or their loved ones threatened.

I have investigated these claims, and met one of these inventors. He was paranoid about being watched, and trusted nobody. His invention was to be transported to Auckland, and he paid a private investigator to track its journey. His stress levels were extreme, and he too, went quiet. He did offer me advice on my invention that showed me that he knew what he was talking about.

I heard a story from a reputable source about a J1 Bedford truck that had two fuel tanks attached to it; one with petrol, and one with water. A man dissolved a large white pill into the water tank. The motor was started on the petrol tank and, when it was up to temperature, it was changed over to the water tank. It continued to run.

I had an old lawn mower, and for several years I tried to get it to run on water. I was worried about making a bomb and hurting myself, so was cautious, but I came to the conclusion that; running on 20% water was relatively easy, 50% was achievable and 70% theoretically possible. It's unlikely to be economical to run a motor on these concoctions as the added chemicals cost a lot more than petrol, but it is still a project that I would like to complete, or see completed.

Magnetism

The humble fridge magnet is amazing! It uses energy, hanging onto the fridge year-after-year, without losing any power. If you use this magnet to magnetise another piece of steel, it actually makes the original magnet stronger!

If someone discovers something that can block magnetic force, without being attracted to it, please let me know!

Water Properties

70% of our earth is made up of ocean water. A baby's body is made up of 78% water; by the time it is one-year-old, this percentage drops to about 65%. In adult men, about 60% of their bodies are water. It would be hard to be unaware, of how important water is, in our lives. There are three different forms of water, or H_2O: solid (ice), liquid (water), and gas (steam). Because water seems so ubiquitous, many people are unaware of its unusual and unique properties.

Despite its small molecular weight, water has an incredibly high boiling point. This is because water requires more energy to break its hydrogen bonds, before it can then begin to boil. The same concept can be applied to freezing point as well. The boiling and freezing points of water enable the molecules to boil or freeze very slowly, which is important to the ecosystems living in water. If it was very easy to freeze or boil water, the resulting drastic changes in the environment, including the oceans and lakes would cause all the organisms that live in water to die. This is also the reason why our sweat cools our bodies.

Besides mercury, water has the highest surface tension of all liquids. Water's high surface tension is due to the hydrogen bonding in water molecules. Water also has an exceptionally high vaporisation temperature.

All substances, including water, become less dense when they are heated and denser when they are cooled. When water is cooled, it becomes denser and forms ice. Water is one of the few substances that can float, in its solid state, on its liquid state. Why? Water continues to become denser, until it reaches 4°C. After it reaches 4°C, it becomes LESS dense.

It is very rare to find a compound lacking carbon that can be in its liquid form at standard temperatures and pressures. Therefore, it is unusual for water to be in its liquid state, at room temperature!

Because of water's polarity, it is able to dissolve or dissociate many particles. Oxygen has a slightly negative charge, while the two hydrogens have a slightly positive charge.

There are many more interesting facts about water that could fill a book on its own, and I am sure that it could be used in many more ways than it is being used currently. That is why it is an integral part of my perpetual-motion energy generator, and the reason I want to run my lawn mower on it!

Basic Principle

Apart from the characteristics listed above, water is an anti-gravitational device. If, for example, a 20-metre-high vertical pipe was filled with water and a ping pong ball was placed in the bottom, the ball would rise rapidly to the top. If it then popped out of the pipe, gravity would pull it down to almost where it started from.

If a magnet was then placed into the ball, and a coil of wire wound around the pipe, it would produce electricity, going both up and down. The secret is, to transfer the ball from the air to the water, using less power than it would generate going up and down.

Obviously, you would not use a ping pong ball, or start with a 20-meter pipe, but this illustrates the basic principle.

Seven

School

School was a 'mixed bag' for me. When I started in 1965, we still had school milk delivered and used ink cartridge pens. Being left-handed would often make things difficult; especially when I was learning to write. A right-handed person is able to pivot at the elbow and produce an even slope, but a left-hander has to push and pull, causing the letters to go all over the place. At least, they did that for me, anyway!

Wet ink pens made it even worse, as your hand would smudge the previous writing. The nib of the pen would catch and grab and leave blotches of ink. I never did get it sorted, even with ball point pens, and I spent many hours re-writing assignments, so that teachers could read them.

I wrote my first poem when I was six-years-old:

> Cars are better than people
> Because they can go fast
> And people can't go as far
> Because their feet don't last!

I soon learned that writing a poem used fewer words per line than a story. So when asked to write a story, I would often write a poem instead. It was generally good enough to get away with it! I have primary school reports saying that I wrote outstanding poetry.

For a time, on Monday mornings, we had to write "What I did on the weekend." My mother saved many of these stories, along with my poems, so I have a snapshot in time of some of the things I did as a young boy.

Ironically, through all of my schooling, some of my highest and lowest marks were for English, as I often ignored the basic rules for punctuation, spelling and grammar.

Bullies

I don't know why some kids get picked on by bullies at school, but I was one of them. Maybe it was the horrible haircuts my father gave me with hand cutters; maybe it was because I didn't swear like the others; maybe it was the old clothes I wore, or maybe it was because I was no good at any sport. Later on, the heavy-rimmed glasses wouldn't have helped! It was likely to be a combination of all of the above.

At primary school, the bullies' challenge was to make me cry. They would throw me into prickle patches and gorse bushes, or squirt me with acid from water pistols. They would ankle-tap me when I was running and shove my face into the ground, or punch me repeatedly in the ribcage, while they had me in a head lock.

Once, at intermediate school, they put a trip wire across the classroom doorway, and I hit my head on a desk on the way down.

This gave me delayed concussion and resulted in an overnight stay in Wellington Hospital.

Mana College was about 15 km from home, so I used to catch the bus. They would sometimes sit beside me, squash me against the side of the bus and punch me again-and-again, in my side and stomach. Sometimes they would throw my school bag out of the moving bus window, and I would have to get off at the next stop to recover my bag and walk the rest of the way home. When I stopped using the bus, cycling to school instead, regardless of wind or rain; I would find my bike tyres let down or the chain pulled off, but I don't think that was too often. I bought my Honda-50 scooter when I was 14 and even before I had my licence, I started riding it to school. I don't remember that ever being sabotaged, but I do remember getting pelted with eggs and other food when slowing down for the corner by the sports' ground.

Then there was the verbal abuse! My parents would say, *"Sticks and stones may break my bones, but names can never hurt me!"* That is so wrong! Physical wounds can heal, but verbal abuse can have serious, long-term consequences.

I had a 'buddy' for a couple of years, who acted as my minder. He was Sri Lankan and, when I first met him, he had a very limited understanding of English. When Wasanta (I think his name was) first started at my school, I was buddied up with him, as some of the kids were cruel to him too. He once asked one of the bullies, the name of a teacher. He was told that his name was Mr Dickhead, and they stood back and watched the reaction, as Wasanta called out to that teacher: "Mr Dickhead!"

Wasanta was apparently, invincible. He would tell us to hit him as hard as we could in the stomach, or bend his fingers back and he would just smile at us. We were walking from Mana College to the Porirua shops one time, when four boys approached us with knives. Wasanta stood in front of me and smiled at them! After the first two lunged at him, only to find themselves knifeless with sore arms, the other two ran off.

So what effect did this have on me? No one ever saw me cry. I cried on the inside, but always managed to hide it on the outside. I can remember fighting back on three occasions: once I got a boy in a headlock and nearly choked him; another time, I repeatedly punched a boy in the head, until I was pulled off; and when I was at Mana College, I shoved a boy's head through a glass window. All the other times I was bullied, I think I just took it.

It was probably about ten years before I could sit comfortably on a bus again. I would walk out of picture theatres if I had to sit next to a stranger, and I would always sit at the end of a row of seats, even at a church service.

My twitches were the most obvious thing. I had periods of rapid blinking, for a few years, and uncontrollable jaw movements. The head twitches still occur, 40 years later, but less severe and less frequent than before.

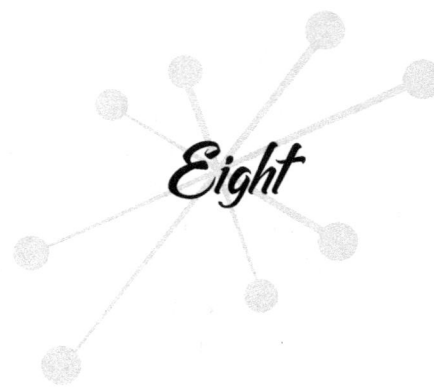

Eight

Depression

I've suffered several bouts of depression over many years, some to the point of being suicidal. Some of this may be due to chemical imbalance, as there is a history of it on both sides of my family.

Sometimes, there is a good reason for it, but most times, there is no logic to it at all. At my worst, I can barely work or drive. Something as simple as finding the centre of a room and putting a light there will become a big task, and then I would lose sleep at night, wondering if I tightened the screws properly!

There was one time, I was driving down a street and I saw a lady getting chased out of a property, by a large, angry dog. I instantly stopped my van and jumped out to go rescue her. My logic was that, if I got mauled to death, I would die a hero, and my family would get the life insurance! The owner called the dog back before I got there.

Another time, I went to see a doctor and he gave me a prescription for the strongest sleeping pills available. It was like he had given me a loaded gun. I now had the means to kill myself painlessly and it would've probably been classed as an accidental overdose.

Sometimes, the light at the end of the tunnel is ever so dim, but I have to keep focused on it. One thing that keeps me going is my family. I am very loved by my children, my grandchildren, and my wife.

Medication has probably saved my life and I always have it on standby, but I don't like the side effects and try to avoid it as much as possible.

The best counselling advice I was given is to have some 'me' time every day. Go for a walk, or just stop and read a car magazine, or do something I enjoy for a time each day.

Nine

Te Reo Maori

When I moved to Gisborne at 17, I could not count to ten in Maori.

Growing up, I used to talk about "Nutty Toa Marees, what a funny name!" I lived in 'Tee Tie' Bay, not Titahi Bay, and many other names were mispronounced. It must have been highly insulting to Maori, but I didn't know any different at the time. This may have contributed to the bullying at school.

Even today, it is very common for the mispronunciation of many Maori words and place names. Even radio and television will say: farnow, instead of whanau; Towerpoe, instead of Taupo; Whyrower, instead of Wairoa; just to mention a few. I don't believe we all need to learn Te Reo Maori, but I think we all should make the effort to at least pronounce the words correctly, especially the place names.

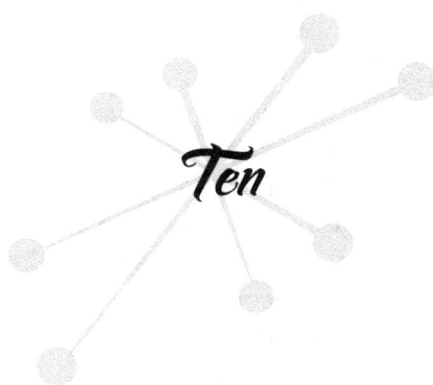

Ten

Mischief Years

Our 'naughty fun' was quite harmless really. In the 1970s, the travel shops had life-sized, cardboard cut-outs of Selwyn Toogood in front of their shops. We 'kidnapped' Selwyn, carried him back to Mana College, and placed him in the principal's office chair!

Our youth group would regularly go into Wellington City for things like ten pin bowling or roller skating. Our drivers would turn the windscreen-washer 'squirters' toward the footpath and squirt selected pedestrians as we drove past!

We would get a long piece of string, attach a handle to one end, and look for a person standing by a corner. We would then ask them if they would mind holding on to the handle for us and to please, not let go. The other end was taken around the corner, tied to a lamp post, rubbish bin, or something, and then we would watch from a distance, to see how long they would hang on before they walked around the corner!

Guy Fawkes'

Guy Fawkes' used to be a lot of fun, for an extended period of time.

We would mix-and-match and make multi-stage rockets. We made long fuses, so that we could blow up gliders in flight, and boats on the water. We made a 'Guy' out of old newspaper and clothing, stuffed with fireworks and placed it in an old pram. This was pushed through the shopping centre with a money box and we would call out: "penny for the Guy." People would give us loose change.

The 5th of November, or the nearest Saturday, would be 'bonfire' time at the beach, and the Guy would be thrown on it, to be blown up.

One Guy Fawkes', we were walking around with packets of Double Happys fireworks, letting them off in different locations and containers, to hear the different sounds that they made. We put some of them into a rubbish bin, outside a fish-and-chip shop and, after hearing the dull boom; we saw puffs of smoke coming out. When more smoke appeared and we saw the first flame, we knew it was time to run! We ran up the hill and hid in the bushes to watch. It was quite impressive how quickly the fire engine arrived, to put it out! Fortunately, it only resulted in a blackened rubbish bin.

Sadly, there were (and are), too many thoughtless idiots out there, and many people and animals have suffered terribly, not to mention, far worse fires than a rubbish bin! As much as I would like the old crackers back, I think all public sales should be banned; organised displays only, and we should find something else to celebrate!

Some have suggested, and I agree with the idea, that the 'Battle at Parihaka' in the 1800's should be celebrated in New Zealand, instead of Guy Fawkes'.

Eleven

Parihaka

Under the leadership of Te Whiti and Tohu, Parihaka Māori began a ploughing campaign, to protest against European settlement, on land confiscated from Māori. Located on the lower slopes of Mt Taranaki, near Cape Egmont, Parihaka became a centre of peaceful resistance from the mid-1860s. The movement involved not only neighbouring tribes, but Māori from around the country. At Parihaka, Te Whiti-o-Rongomai and Tohu Kākahi, began the campaign to resist the settlement of Europeans on the land had been confiscated from the South Taranaki Māori, who had fought against the government.

This campaign used non-violent methods. In 1879, the government started surveying confiscated land on the Waimate plain, south-east of Parihaka. Te Whiti's followers disrupted these surveys by ploughing and fencing land occupied by settlers. Many were arrested and held without trial in the South Island, but the protests continued.

In November 1881, the government sent more than 1500 troops, to Parihaka. Most of its inhabitants were arrested, or driven away; Te Whiti and Tohu were imprisoned until 1883, and the village was demolished. Despite the absence of its leaders, Parihaka was rebuilt. Ploughing campaigns, and arrests without trial of protestors, continued into the 1890s.

Twelve

Bikes

Dad had little mechanical ability; I don't think he ever replaced a spark plug, but he could fix pushbikes; a throwback from his youth, when he would cycle for miles and had no one to fix his bikes for him. He found three old bikes and fixed one up for my sister, and two for me.

We had a dog for a couple of years, named Paddy. He was a Pug-Pekinese-cross. The doctor said that he had to go, because of my sister's asthma.

One Saturday morning, Dad was fixing one of the bikes. He had taken the bearings out, which were covered in grease. Dad had placed them in a bowl, but Paddy must have liked the taste of grease, because he ate them all! He was confined to the basement, on a short lead, until they passed through, and Dad could get them back!

My first bike was way, too big for me. I couldn't sit on the seat and reach the pedals, even on the lowest position. My lesson on road rules was: always keep left, and put my arm out to indicate, every time I went around a corner. Mum tied a ribbon on the left handlebar, so I knew which side had to be closest to the footpath. They didn't tell me that I only had to indicate when I was at an intersection, or that I could stop indicating partway around the turn. So here I was on my oversized bike; not sitting on the seat, going around every corner with only one hand on the handlebars and the other sticking straight out, until I completed the turn!

They didn't have BMX or mountain bikes back then, but if they had, I would have been a brilliant rider! As I got older, I could jump up large steps, do wheel stands and, even balance, on the front wheel. I buckled several front forks doing jumps, and all of this, on a heavy Raleigh roadster!

I can remember talking to the man in the motorbike shop (who used to give me free posters), about putting pedals on a small motorbike frame, or putting a motorbike front end on a pushbike. He said that it would make it too heavy, but we did contemplate the possibility of grafting-in front telescopic forks. If only we had followed through with the idea and marketed it!

Later, I got a 5-speed, touring bike from an Englishman that brought the bike to New Zealand with him. It had 5-speed hub gears, like the Sturmey Archer, but with an extra-high and extra-low ratio; wider rims, with wider straight tread tyres; and a leather seat. Unfortunately, the tyres weren't available in New Zealand, so I had to fit standard tyres when they wore out. On a flat road with a tail wind, I could reach 50kph, and on a long steep hill I reached 110kph with a pace-car behind me, to confirm it!

In 1975, I went on an organised bike tour from Gisborne to Whakatane, via the coast road. I had traveled with my bike on the train to the Gisborne starting point. We had a support car to carry tents and cooking gear, etc; but I think it rained, from start to finish! By the time the bike and I arrived back at Porirua Railway Station, the bike had been stripped of its seat, mirrors, headlight and horn; quite typical of New Zealand Railways in those days! They had a standard pay-out for damage claims, regardless of what the parts were worth.

Many years later, while a single parent, I would find many unused bikes in sheds and backyards, and fix them up, as a hobby. Most of them were given away. One time, my son got a puncture, so I tried to get him to fix it. He said that it would take too long, so I got him to time me. It was fixed and he was riding the bike in less than five minutes!

Wellington Winds

Cycling to school, in Wellington winds, was often a challenge! Head winds would mean an even lower gear on the Honda 50, and a very low gear, on the bike! I thought of making a sail, to catch the tail winds, but the direction never seemed to stay constant.

My sister, Irene and I, would play a game on the windy days. We would follow the fence line up a hilly, farm paddock, let go at the top, and see who could stand up the longest, without hanging on! We would lean into the wind one way, and then a gust would come from the other direction, and flatten us!

Thirteen

Trains

My grandfather, on my father's side, spent his whole working life in the railways. In 1964, he was the station master at the Paekakariki Railway Station, when one of the last steam trains came through. My dad took me for a visit and Poppa, (as I called him), held me up to ring the bell, to signal for the train to depart from the station. The AB Loco let out a deafening toot and a hiss of steam that sent me scarpering to the other side. I was both frightened and fascinated at the same time!

This was the start of a lifelong fascination with trains, or perhaps it was the story books that my mum used to read to me at bed time; 'The Little Red Caboose,' or 'The Little Engine that Could.' Maybe it was the song, 'I've been working on the Railroad, all my live long day'.

When I was eight years old, my parents bought me my first Triang-Hornby train set. It had an engine, three carriages, a caboose, and a small, oval track. For the next ten years, buying me something for Christmas or birthdays was never a problem, as they just had to buy something for the train set, and I was happy!

Dad made me a six-foot by nine-foot (2m x 3m) board in the basement to set the train up on, and many happy hours were spent making fences out of matchsticks; buildings out of matchboxes; and papier-mâché hills and tunnels.

When I was a single parent, we rented a large house with two lounge areas, so the train got a permanent position inside the house. At its peak, I had 12 engines and 46 carriages. I used to be a care-giver for a lot of children, so it got very well-used. Unfortunately, it got quite damaged as well. If the train de-railed on the far side, for instance; children would climb on and over to get it, crushing everything under them!

I eventually downsized it, putting any valuable bits into storage, so this wasn't a worry. When I got the Internet and found 'Trademe', I sold a lot off. One of the ongoing problems was the metal track that constantly needed cleaning for good electrical contact. The engines also had magnets in them that gave 'Magnitraction' that produced enough traction to pull heavy loads. Today, they have non-ferrous track and electronic controllers that work far better! A couple of years ago I started re-building with this new track in my home brew shed. I designed a spiral track and am enjoying the train again!

Recently, I picked up four sets of G-gauge railway as well. This has 45mm plastic track and battery-powered engines, with remote control. This is also known as garden-gauge, as it can be set up outside. I have enough track for a complete loop of the entire length of the house, but I'm not sure what its final use will be!

I once had a friend who was a train driver in Wellington, and he would take me with him on Sunday afternoons to drive the trains. We would only do short shunts of maybe 30 or 40 metres, but I could say I have driven a DA and DX loco and a railcar! The engines had explosives in a box that could be put on the track, and they would make a very loud bang when run over, as an emergency warning device. Of course we had to try them out!

I joined a railway enthusiast club and made a few trips back to Paekakariki, to help with steam engine restoration. When I left school, joining the railways was high on my option list, but Dad regarded them as a 'den of iniquity'. He had very bad memories of being a 'railway child' himself, so working there couldn't happen.

After moving to Gisborne I lost my connection to trains, other than making return trips by rail, until a slip closed the link. This was due to a serious lack of maintenance, on what was an uneconomical line. Not long before closure, local Gisborne companies invested a considerable amount of money to increase rail traffic. The longer this line remains closed, the more it will cost to re-open and the longer it will take to make it economical.

This is, by far, the most beautiful stretch of railway I have ever been on and I am certain it could become quite economical in the long term. Gisborne still has its WA165 steam-loco and carriages and does regular excursions to Muriwai, but it used to do the beach loop further over the Whareratas, before the slip.

I haven't had a lot of input into WA165's restoration and running, but I have published a book (in poetic form) on its history, and donate nearly all the profits from its sales, into its running.

Fourteen

Cars

A friend's older brother was a motor mechanic and he cut the body off a Vanguard, made a roll cage, and fitted large wheels to the back. This created a 'dune buggy' that was raced around on the beach and in grass paddocks. The motor seized, so I was asked if I wanted it. Mum did not know what a dune buggy was, but thought it was the size of a go-cart. After saying that I could have it, she was very shocked when this very rusty vehicle got towed over by a very noisy V8 Chevy! I was the happiest 14-year-old around!

Dad bought me a 3/8th drive socket set and, with a 12 inch crescent and a few screwdrivers, I dismantled the entire engine. It was never going to go again, but I bought the 'Mechanics of the Motor Vehicle' apprentice training manual and identified every part, and how it worked. I was keen to be a mechanic, but an older mechanic friend of mine, advised me to keep it as a hobby, as the novelty of working on cars wears off when you are doing it every day. Some of the best advice I have been given! Eventually, everything was sold, given away or dumped.

I got my driver's licence not long after I turned 15. Dad gave me driving lessons when I was 14 and then I had two lessons with a driving school, so that I could use their vehicle to sit the test. I drove through an intersection, did a hill start, a 3-point turn, parallel parked, paid $10, and was given a temporary, full driver's licence, until the permanent one arrived in the post.

Dad's car, at the time, was an HC Vauxhall Viva. They didn't have a great reputation, but it was a remarkably good car at the time. I was rally driving it, on a gravel farm road with my mate once, when I slid off the road and put a hole in the exhaust. Copious amounts of chewing gum was chewed and moulded in and around the hole, but with limited results. Tea towels tended to catch on fire, so I had to resort to pleading ignorance as to how it got damaged!

The Honda 50 that I mentioned in an earlier chapter was bought off a motor mechanic; it had a bigger 'carb' and a modified exhaust. I would ride it to the max, often having the foot pedals sparking off the tarmac.

One trip I was visiting a friend in Levin, and on the return trip, I had a strong tail wind. Riding as I did, on full throttle, I was going faster than the theoretical top speed, when the bike started getting slower and slower, until it came to a halt. I jumped on the kick start to try and restart it, but the shaft broke. I checked the oil, to find it boiling in the sump. The motor was seized! It took me several hours to push it home, and then a few weeks to strip and rebuild the engine!

Cars and motors were always high on the interest list for me. I would go to the annual Speed Boat Regatta held on the Porirua Harbour, and apart from the racing, I would look over every tow-car; the Mustangs, Monaros, Chargers, etc; taking note of how high the speedos would read up to.

My mate had a 100E Ford Prefect. We decided it was too quiet, so we drilled holes in the muffler to make it sound better! We didn't quite get the sound we wanted, but I think it made it go even slower! He later put a 1200cc Cortina motor in it with a Webber 'carb' that made it go better!

We were rally driving the Prefect over a gravel road and slid into a fence; knocking the right front guard into the wheel. Fortunately we had a tow rope in the boot, which we tied around the bumper and guard, and onto a fencepost; then drove backwards, as fast and straight as possible! The bumper bent back slightly, but the fencepost broke, at ground level, flattening a section of fence! We managed to get the car to a power pole and repeated the exercise. This time, the pole didn't move and the steering was back to normal, but the bumper and front guard had been torn off!

Another friend had a Mark 2 Ford Zephyr. He fitted a V8 Mustang motor into it and put fat tyres on the back. It still had the original diff, so it had very low gearing. After a couple of runs to check it was going o.k., he decided to check its maximum acceleration. We found a long straight road with coarse seal, for maximum grip. He revved it out and dropped the clutch. The front lifted in the air like a dragster, lifting the front wheels off the ground. Then it crashed down, the standard suspension buckling under the weight, and the already-low sump collecting the road; bending the oil pickup into the big end; and bringing everything to a sudden halt, in a pool of oil!

I've owned over a hundred cars myself, sometimes five or six at a time. I enjoyed the challenge of finding cars parked up that hadn't gone for a long time, and getting them going. Quite a few ended up in demolition derbies at the speedway, a pastime my brother and I enjoyed for quite a few years.

My Isuzu Bellett was a remarkable car for its time. It had cross-ply tyres when I bought it, but I got a pair of radials and experimented with them, on the back and front. On the back, you could induce gross understeer driving hard into a corner. However, with them on the front, it would be the opposite, with the back sliding all over the place, but the front would pretty-well stay pointing in the right direction. I eventually got radials all round and it was a remarkably good handling car!

For some strange reason I let my younger brother, Phil, borrow the Isuzu from time to time. It came home with a big dent in the back one time, but he did a remarkably, good job straightening it out. It wasn't his fault, as he stopped but the car behind didn't. I found out later that he used to push the car to the limits, even more than I did!

I've always hated cars following too close. I was going down a hill one time, with a car following right up my bumper, so I pulled the handbrake on, rapidly slowing without the brake lights showing. His car was worth more than mine and if he hit me, it would have been his fault. He got awfully close and then went into a slide, with smoke coming off the tyres as he panic-braked! I would have felt terrible if he had hurt himself, but I'm sure that he wished he had kept his distance!

I had my 1969 P6 Rover 2000 for about ten years. It was the 'single-carb' version, but I bored it out, fitted high compression pistons, electronic ignition and various exhaust systems.

My first Japanese-import was a Mitsubishi Delica 1800cc van.

I got it cheap, but it was blowing a lot of smoke. I found that the later model vans used basically the same motor as the Sigma, so I got a 2-litre 4G63 motor; bored it out 20-thou, fitted a hot cam and extractors, and put it in my van. It was almost a straight swap, but the dipstick was always in the wrong place! It went very well and wheel-spin was easily induced!

It always had rust problems that were un-stoppable, but I sold it with a new W.O.F. and the new owner gave it back after six months! It made a good mobile shed and it was very fortuitous that I kept it, because a few years later, I 'inherited' a Mitsubishi Starion-turbo that blew its motor on a trip back from Wellington. It needed a new head and I found it was identical, so a swap from van-to-Starion got it going again!

One of my better buys was a Nissan Sunny, an early front wheel-drive version. I was given one for nothing, so I looked for another, for parts. I found one that had been parked up for about two years, and got it for the price of the new tyres that had been put on. After towing it home; I cleaned the cobwebs out of the 'carb'; put in fresh petrol and a battery; and it started and ran beautifully! It only needed a brake adjustment for a warrant! I kept it for several years and then sold it and bought it back, twice.

The most fun car I have owned was a Mitsubishi Mirage, with the super-shift manual gearbox. I bought it off a bloke that had done it up for use with the Gisborne Car Club, so it had a hot motor and very stiff suspension. The custom exhaust gave it a really nice tone! Very few cars could out pace it on a winding road!

In the 1980s I bought a Mazda Capella RX2-rotary. It had stage-2 engine modifications on a 12A motor. It was like driving a 1600cc under 3000 RPM and then, when it came into its power band, was like a V8! It didn't handle particularly well with variable-ratio, re-circulating ball steering and bad spring and damper settings, but it had a mint body and interior, and no rust. At the time, people were throwing the rotary motor away and transplanting 4-cylinder 1600s to improve the terrible fuel-economy and engine-wear. If I had the same car now, I could sell it and retire on the earnings!

At the time of writing this in 2018, my only vehicle—other than my Mazda MPV work vehicle, is my 1958 Morris Minor, which I've owned for 22 years. I had a budget of $1000 at the time, to have a road-legal Minor on the road. For my $1000, I bought three Morris Minors: an unfinished restoration project that was to be the base car; a rusted, parts car that was still in the system; and a 1969 van that was very rusted, but had the later-model parts; like the 1100cc motor, larger front brakes, wider rims, etc.

As I worked for the power board, the fault-men knew where, just about, every Morris Minor was parked up; in paddocks and back yards, from Wairoa to East Cape, so I would go on weekends exploring. I would raid parts, or get whole cars, and would have up to five at any one time.

I kept blowing gearboxes and a friend from the Rotorua Morris Minor Club, said that he had a friend, who made conversion kits to fit a Toyota 5-speed gearbox, at a good price. This took quite a few months to arrive and I found that, almost nothing fitted as it should. The car itself was showing serious rust problems and I was a single parent at the time, with no spare money.

To cut a long story short, I had no mobile car for about six years. In that time, I picked up a 1275 Morris Marina motor, which is the largest A-series motor that can be easily transplanted. After moving house, (a huge undertaking at the time, considering my large accumulation of valuable assets) I made the drastic decision to sell everything and maybe, buy a good M.G. later, when I had spare money again.

I got a good price for the Marina motor, but decided that the rest would not earn much money as it was not a going concern; all the parts were in unknown condition, having sat around for so long. The motor was bored out with an electric drill and honing tool, and I mixed-and-matched engine parts to get it running.

There are few small 4-cylinder motors that sound better than an A-series; with long centre-branch extractors, a hot camshaft and a custom free-flow exhaust system. When I heard that crispy growl again, my passion for the project was re-ignited. Another house-move was looming; so more assets were disposed of, but the Morris was, this time, driven to its new location. By this time, I was engaged and fortunately my creative fiancée was a willing participant; making new seat covers from period-correct, heavy curtain material and suggesting that we get it finished to use as a wedding car!

Our wedding car it was, with Ani and I arriving together at the church with our Collie, Ema. It had got a quick paint re-spray by me in the back yard, but had hardly any brakes. The exhaust was tied on with wire, and had serious rust issues underneath.

Even after my major clean-outs, the Morris would just not fit into the double garage after my move to our current Aberdeen Rd house! Eventually, I could push it in and pull it out, but couldn't open doors whilst inside. It took several more years to get the car road legal and to be able to drive in and out.

Morris in shed

Current specifications: 1100cc bored-out 60-thou. Raised compression. Road/Race cam with longer duration and higher lift. MG/Cooper S 295 head, twin carbs, extractors, custom exhaust with sports muffler. Electronic ignition and sport's coil, Toyota 5-speed gearbox and clutch. Telescopic rear shocks. Stiffened and Nolathene-bushed front suspension. Have twin-throat 40 DCOE Webber carb with K+N filter that I fit occasionally, for better performance.

The parts' car was stored at a friend's paddock out in the country, and I wanted to bring it into town. As Ani is a horticulturist, (amongst other things) we agreed to put it on the front lawn and plant flowers in it as a garden feature. After towing and pushing it into place, we rust-proofed the doors and body, and gave it a repaint in deep blue. The bonnet and head were removed and we fitted plant boxes into the engine-bay and side windows. The headlamps have 230 volt fridge bulbs that turn on with a timer, and at Christmas time it gets lit up with coloured lights. It has become a Gisborne icon and has been featured in the local newspaper.

Garden parts' car

When I was at the power board in the 1980s, I can remember the steel-belted, radial tyres coming out. The general opinion was: 'don't buy them', because they give a harsh ride and they don't retread well, so you would need to buy a new tyre when the tread wears down!

There was also the opinion that you shouldn't buy a new Toyota, because you can't give them a valve grind and so, would need to buy a whole new head if the valves burnt out! In later years, I bought an ex-taxi Toyota Hi-Ace that had done over 800,000 kilometres! I was going for the million, but the rust got to it first.

How do you know when it's time to stop working on your classic and go inside? When you're working on the brakes, and you've just realised that you've spent the last 20-minutes, trying to bleed a grease nipple!

Vehicle Registration

The vehicle continuous-registration scheme and the fact that you cannot register your car without a WOF, is a money-making scam! If your WOF runs out and you just want to register your vehicle until repairs are made, they won't let you. If you then get a ticket from an officer or council parking warden; it will be for no 'rego', as well as no WOF. When you then get your WOF and re-register, they insist that you pay for the back period of the 'rego' that you just got the fine for not having! One minute they refuse to take your money, and the next, they insist on taking it, for the same thing!

If you put your vehicle registration on hold and then forget to renew the suspension on time, the money metre starts ticking again. You may forget all about it until you get a letter a year later, asking for hundreds of dollars for back registration, for a vehicle that has never moved.

The current WOF system is good in theory, but that too has cost me a lot of unnecessary money over the years; as the inspectors can often get it wrong, and there is no system in place to permit disputes, or even to get another opinion. I had a broken window-winder for the driver's window one time, so I left the window down until I could get it fixed. They failed the WOF check because they couldn't see the safety glass logo on the glass! The most stupid thing that they insist on 'having working' on a car, is the park lights! When do you use them? If you park your car, for more than a few minutes, with the park lights on, you will get a flat battery!

Traffic officers have also cost me a lot of money! Once, I had been to the beach with the kids; one of them had put the seat back, and laid a towel over her and her seatbelt. When the officer pulled me over, she put the seat back upright, and the towel fell off. The officer insisted that she hadn't been wearing a belt and that she had just put it on then. When I insisted that she had been wearing it all the time, the officer said that because I argued about it, I was getting a ticket; otherwise, I might have been let off with a warning! When I disputed the fine in writing, they just said that my story was different to that of the officer!

My second no-seatbelt fine was less than a year later, when an officer pulled me over for not completely stopping at a stop sign. As soon as I saw him accelerating behind me; I pulled over; flicked my seat belt off; pulled my wallet out of my back pocket; and got out my licence to show him. This time, I didn't dispute not fully stopping, but that I was moving so slowly that there was no risk of a problem. He agreed to give me a warning only for not stopping, but said that he was giving me a ticket for not wearing a seatbelt! I told him that I had taken it off to get my licence out of my wallet, but he insisted that I had not been wearing it, when he pulled in behind me! My letter of explanation got the same response as last time!

The current policy of traffic officers calling off pursuits if the fleeing vehicle is driving dangerously, is definitely not working! The offender knows that if he drives fast and dangerously enough, he has a chance of getting away. This is causing a lot of offenders to crash and kill, or seriously injure themselves or others. The policy needs to be, that the police will pursue, no matter what; so don't bother trying to run!

The proposed experiment

I would love to carry out an experiment. I would choose 500 people from throughout New Zealand, after looking into: past driving record and experience; a current road trip and interview; and checking current vehicles that they are likely to drive. I would then tell them that for the next 12 months, all road rules are optional and they will get no fines for any infringement. Here is what I would expect to happen:

- All of them would obey the basic rules like; wearing seatbelts, obeying traffic lights and giving way.
- Most would exceed the speed limit by a modest amount, both in town and on the open road, but only in areas where they would consider it safe to do so.
- Some would not fully stop at some stop signs, and would sometimes, cross over the centreline, when driving on winding roads; again, when they had good visibility and considered it safe to do so.
- Some might drive after consuming alcohol, but it would likely be at the lower end and they would drive a short distance, slowly and carefully.
- All would keep their vehicles up to Warrant of Fitness standard.
- None of them would be involved in a serious traffic incident.

It's interesting that vehicle crashes are generally referred to as accidents, when very few of them are accidental. Most of them are the result of somebody making a bad decision. I know that if I am tired; under emotional stress, driving in glare, rain, on unfamiliar roads at night, or in heavy traffic—my risk of having an incident rises considerably. It is unfortunate that regardless of extensive advertising campaigns; not wearing seatbelts, excessive alcohol consumption and speeding are still the main contributing factors to vehicle-related injuries and death. Sometimes, something as simple as checking a vehicle's tyre pressures, could save someone's life.

There is a defect in every new car made, that nobody is allowed to correct. That is speedo error. Every speedo will read a higher speed than the car is travelling. This is to prevent car companies from being sued.

Fifteen

Smoking

When I was about 12 or 13 years old, I found a packet of cigarette papers. I had heard that people got high from smoking grass, so I thought I would give it a try. Green, lawn grass did not smoke well, so I guessed I got it wrong. Observing that tobacco was brown, I came to the correct assumption that the 'grass' had to be dried. To save time, I found some grass in a drain that was already brown, so I tried to smoke that. Again, it was very unpleasant.

I later found out that they actually smoke weed, not grass, but as I had no idea which weeds they smoked, I decided to put the whole idea aside. By the time I tried smoking real cigarettes, I had contact lenses and the smoke seemed to get in my eyes and irritate them. I tried again in my early 20s; to be rebellious and look cool, but I never got any pleasure out of it, so it was short lived.

Sixteen

Politics

Politicians!
Pompous politicians
Postulating on poverty
While practicing polygamy
With their cars and palaces!

I don't follow politics very closely, and normally I don't have strong opinions about the decisions that are made. I trust the politicians to know best and to make wise decisions. In hindsight, some very bad decisions have been made! For example:

Rob Muldoon

15 December 1975 was the day that Rob Muldoon announced the abolition of the compulsory New Zealand Superannuation Scheme that had been introduced by the previous Labour

government. The scheme was innovative and well ahead of its time. It would be worth more than $240 billion today, and would have transformed the New Zealand economy into a world beater.

New Zealand Rail

In 1993, New Zealand Rail Ltd was sold to a business consortium led by an American railway company and a local firm of investment advisers for $328 million. It subsequently became Tranz Rail Ltd and was listed on the New Zealand sharemarket, as well as the NASDAQ in the United States. Ten years later, it was on the brink of receivership, after being run into the ground; the owners walked away with the profits.

The business was then bought by an Australian logistics company, Toll Holdings, and in 2008, it was sold back to the government. Before all this happened, the railway employed over 20,000 people. It was horribly inefficient, but was used, along with other state owned enterprises, to keep the unemployment levels down.

Employment Contracts Act

In 1991, the Employment Contracts Act made union membership voluntary; allowing anyone to bargain on behalf of workers. Employees could choose to work under either an individual, or a collective employment contract, which affected only the specific employers or employees who signed the agreements.

Unions had no special status in the process, because the ECA promoted direct bargaining between the employer and the employee. If they could not agree, the dispute went to an employment tribunal and, if necessary, to an employment court.

By 1999 the tribunal had a backlog of over 3,000 cases, so it took up to a year, to deliver a ruling. This resulted in workers doing the same job alongside each other on different wages and conditions, and with a general downward trend, as employers would play one worker against another.

July 1998: Electricity Industry Reform Act 1998

The act required full ownership separation of distribution (lines) businesses, from supply (retail and generation) businesses. The main reasons were; to encourage competition, and to prevent cross-subsidisation of generation and retail, from lines' customers. Did our power prices drop? No! They were never going to! There were now, many CEOs on million dollar salaries wanting to make maximum profit for shareholders, instead of just one or two.

Hydro power generation is very efficient. The initial energy source is free (water and gravity); the copper wires in the generators and power lines do not wear out; so it basically requires a bit of maintenance on bearings, pylons, switches, transformers, etc. The basic generation and distribution system has been around for a long time and has been paid for by the consumer, many times over.

Many ad-campaigns have been encouraging energy efficiency; even quoting how many millions of dollars that we will "save the country", if we change to energy-efficient light bulbs! Nobody wants you to use less power, or is going to thank you if you do. It does not cost less money to distribute less power.

If we all use less power, the businesses will increase charges to maintain their profit margins. The same company that subsidises insulating houses also subsidises the installation of heat pumps.

This means that, you will use more energy to cool your house during summer, as well as heating during winter.

What they do want is to smooth the usage out during the day. It's the peak usage, at breakfast and tea time, including all the heating during winter, which the system has to be built to cope with. This is why the electric hot water systems are on a slightly cheaper controlled rate; so that they can turn the cylinders off at peak usage times.

The 'smart meters' most commonly installed today, record the usage minute-by-minute. In theory, the energy retailer can provide variable charge rates during the day; so that using the dishwasher after 9pm, for instance, would cost less than using it at 7pm; using it at 11 pm, should be even cheaper. Why they don't offer this service, I do not understand, as it would be a win-win.

Rogernomics

Roger Douglas was the Minister of Finance, from 1984 to 1988. The number of New Zealanders estimated to be living in poverty grew by at least 35% between 1989 and 1992. Between 1985 and 1992, the New Zealand economy grew by 4.7%, during the same period in which, the average OECD nation grew by 28.2%.

From 1984 to 1993; inflation averaged 9% per year, New Zealand's credit rating dropped twice, and foreign debt quadrupled. Between 1986 and 1993, the unemployment rate rose from 3.6% to 11%. Approximately 76,000 manufacturing jobs were lost between 1987 and 1992.

One brilliant move that Douglas managed was to introduce G.S.T. to New Zealand, on 1 October, 1986. It forced all shops, businesses and tradesmen to collect tax for the government, at their own time and expense; with severe penalties if they didn't, and no thanks or compensation if they did!

It was, and still is, a significant cost for a small business. It increased living costs for the poorest New Zealanders by more than twice as much as for the rich, because poor people spend more of what they earn. It was so successful that in July 1989, Labour increased it from 10% to 12.5%. National increased it further, to 15% in 2010.

The lowering of the drinking age

In December 1999, the legal drinking age was lowered from 20 to 18. The immediate consequence of this was that 16-year-olds with false I.D. could purchase alcohol from liquor outlets. The seller knew that if they didn't sell to them, the next outlet would. They would use the excuse that these customers had I.D. and looked 18.

Young teens were quick to use their new power and, previously nice neighbours with teenagers, became neighbours-from-hell, as parties raged! There was a long term increase in the risk of 18 and 19-year-olds being involved in car crashes that caused death or injury. This increased risk has become the new norm.

The Emissions' Trading Scheme

In September 2008, the Labour Government introduced the Emissions' Trading Scheme. This was a carbon tax that a business was obliged to pay, for every two tonnes of carbon dioxide equivalent emissions. It was amended again in 2009 and 2012. As with any tax, this is passed down the chain and the consumer ends up paying.

The Education System

Having no children in the education system today, I don't know much about how things work now, but two things stand out. One is the lack of discipline options in the classroom for teachers to deal with troublesome pupils, and the other thing is classroom sizes that have not changed since the 1960s. 30 pupils for one teacher is too many. Every class with this many children should have at least one other adult present at all times, and disruptive pupils should be able to be forcibly removed if required.

Who rules the World?

In theory, democratic governments represent the people and do what is best for them. In practice, all governments have a level of corruption; many have hidden agendas; many are infiltrated by groups like, the Illuminati, Jesuits and Freemasons; and many are being bribed or blackmailed by groups with money and influence. In some countries, a less corrupt dictatorship is better than a corrupt, voted-in government.

Seventeen

The Media

Globally, the media probably has the greatest power and influence over world affairs. Not all news is true and the media often caters to the thirst for scandal and drama. This is exploited by some groups, like terrorist organisations. A classic example of this is the Palestinian attacks against Israel. They pay civilians to protest on the border; sending rockets and fire bombs into Israel from densely populated areas, and then wait for Israel to retaliate. They want maximum, civilian deaths and injuries, inflicted on their own people, to be reported to the world. This gets them international attention and sympathy for their cause. For some reason, the media play into their hands with biased reporting.

Advertising companies utilise known hypnosis techniques to get people to purchase things they don't need and that may be harmful to them.

Eighteen

Our Historical Building

We have a building on our property that is hundreds of years old! It is distinguished by the traditional waka, hanging on the side. This has obviously been restored and updated over the years, causing it to lose many of its original features, but the basic shape and concept remains the same.

The other distinguishing feature is the 'mower' underneath. This used to house its predecessor, the Moa. The Moa was basically a large chicken, and it would walk around the whare, eating the grass and keeping the lawns looking good. When they started getting harder to find, some bloke invented the 'mower' to do the same job. He spelt it differently, to distinguish between the two. Our ancestors didn't like this new 'mower' so much because it didn't lay eggs, didn't have feathers, and you couldn't eat it when it got old.

The early whare didn't have glass windows because the male, cock-rooster Moa, had a very loud crow that could shatter glass. When they became extinct, glass windows could be used.

Rumour has it, (I don't know if it is true or not), that a glass window salesman was saying how no sound from any creature was going to shatter his glass, when a giant bird flew straight into it, smashing it to bits!

Nineteen

The Complaint

Hello, its Kevin Electrician here, I would like to make a complaint about your Marz downlight.

Oh! That's surprising; we have been selling them for years and haven't had a complaint until now. What's the problem?

The box says that they last up to 30,000 hours. That's about three and a half years. I put some in about four years ago and they are still all working fine.

That sounds great! What's the problem?

The lights are never turned off, so I would have expected them to fail by now, but they haven't! It's false advertising on the box! That's about 6,000 hours over its expected life, and none have failed!

Isn't that a good thing?

No! It's bad for business! I expected to have to replace all the lights at least once every four years! If I knew they were going to last this long, I would have used another sort!

I'm sorry about that! I'm not sure what we can do about it.

Well, I think you could probably start by changing the label on the box to warn others that they are not going to get a lot of repeat business replacing them!

O.K. if you hold on for a couple of minutes, I'll have a talk to my boss. Are there any other problems?

Yes! They are too cheap!
Sorry?

They are too cheap! I put 20% mark up on my goods but I'm not making a lot of profit on these lights!

O.K. I'll talk to my boss and get back to you shortly...

Hello! Are you Kevin? This is James the manager here.
Hi James!

My staff tells me you have been having an interesting conversation about our Marz lights!

Yes! They are too cheap and last too long! This is the 21st century. Things are meant to fail and be replaced on a regular basis like most appliances.

Thank you for your feedback! How many lights did you put in?
Ten.

O.K. We would like to offer you ten free lights if you keep us informed as to how long the lights actually last in practice. Are you happy with that?
Sure! That sounds like a great idea! Thank you!

Thank you! It's been a pleasure talking with you! We appreciate your feedback, Have a great day!
You too! Good-bye!

Twenty

The Interview

Hi! We are doing research into people's drinking habits and wondered if you would mind answering a few questions?

Sure! I'm not much of a drinker but am happy to answer a few questions.

How many days a week do you consume alcohol?

Oh, I don't know. It's not as if I mark it on the calendar or anything!

Do you have a few beers on the weekend or the odd wine with a meal?

When I think about it, it's probably about 7 days a week, give or take a bit.

Give or take?

Yep, sometimes more, sometimes less. But they are only part days I drink, it's not as if I'm drinking all day or anything. I don't normally have a beer until after work at about 4.30pm or 5 o'clock unless I knock off early to do paperwork or something, then I might have a beer about 3pm, but if I'm out for lunch or it's the weekend I might have a beer or two with my lunch, as you do.

If it's a hot day and I've just mowed the lawns or something, I might have a beer around 10 o'clock, unless it's a celebration like a wedding or something, I might have an early beer.

Sometimes I put a bit of vodka in my morning coffee to help warm me up and I'll have a few swigs of Jaegermeister during the day but that is medicinal for my throat, so doesn't really count does it?

O.K. has anyone told you; you might have a problem with alcohol?

Oh no! I don't have a problem with alcohol! Alcohol doesn't have a problem with me either, in fact we seem to get along very well together! I can stop drinking any time I want, no problem!

Why don't you?

Cause I never want to! Well actually I did once, a year or two ago. I went without a drink for a day or two. I think I was sick or something but I don't recall it being a problem.

Are you aware of the effects that alcohol can have on your body?

They use it as a cleanser in the hospitals so it can't be too bad for you, besides, by the laws of nature, if it's going to kill off any cells, it will kill the weaker ones first making me stronger!"

It actually greatly increases the chance of you getting liver disease and cancer.

Doesn't everything? If we avoided all the things that might give us cancer, we would never leave the house and probably die of starvation! Besides, it's other people that get that, not me! I'm way too healthy to worry about things like that!

Thank you for talking to us! Do you know where to get help if you need it?

Sure! The Internet! Mr Google has an answer for everything! It's been nice talking to you. Bye!

Twenty-one

Letter to the Editor

Dear Sir,

I received an e-mail from a nice lady a few weeks back, to say that she needed to borrow some money so she could visit her dying father in New Zealand. Apparently she is going to inherit a large amount of money from the estate, and she is going to share it with me for my kindness.

The problem is, that after depositing $10,000 into her foreign bank account, I seem to have lost contact with her. She is a bit backward and I want to make sure that she got to New Zealand o.k.

Her name is Rekcus, from the Russian town of Ekorb. Her Dad's name is Eman Pu-Edam and he is staying at Macs.

If anyone comes across her or her dad, could they please let me know, so that I know they are o.k?

Regards, Di Puts.

(Did you pick up on the backward masking on the names?)

Twenty-two

The Knife

Hi! I have this knife here that has a broken handle. It has a lifetime guarantee and I would like a replacement please.

Do you have the receipt?

No, I bought it a long time ago.

Oh! I'm sorry; we can't replace it without a receipt.

I don't need a receipt. You send it back to the manufacturer and they replace it.

Wait just a minute and I will go see my boss.

(5 minutes later)

How do we know it had a lifetime guarantee when you bought it?

You have them on your shelf and they say lifetime guarantee on the packet. They don't randomly put them on. If it has one now, it would have had one then.

The Knife

Just wait a minute; I'll go see the boss.

(5 minutes later)

Did you buy it from this shop?

No I didn't.

Well, you will have to take it back to the shop you bought it from then.

That shop doesn't exist anymore. You stock them so you can send it back to the manufacturer for replacement.

Just wait a minute, I'll just go see the boss.

(5 minutes later)

What were you doing with the knife when it broke?

I was cutting with it!

What were you cutting?

Steak.

I really don't think you should be using that knife to cut steak, it's not a steak knife you know.

It doesn't matter what I was cutting! There is no exclusion clause for cutting steak!

Wait a minute please; I'll just see the boss again.

(5 minutes later)

How long ago did you buy it?

I'm not sure, probably about 15 years ago.

Well I don't think you will get a replacement for that knife then! It's a lifetime guarantee, not a forever guarantee, and the life of that knife is well over! I wouldn't expect it to last much over ten years!

Look! Just send it back to the manufacturer and let them decide! I'm sure they will happily replace it!

All right! There's no need to get angry with me! I'm just trying to help! If you just wait a couple of minutes, I'll go see the boss and we will see what we can do.

(5 minutes later)

The boss said to just give you a new one off the shelf and we will send the old one back to the manufacturer. That was nice and easy, wasn't it! Is there anything else I can help you with?

No! Thank you. Goodbye!

Twenty-three

Modern Technology

Life today has many benefits and things that really annoy me!

Battery-powered tools are the greatest thing for tradesmen! There are no more trailing power cords on the floor.

L.E.D. lighting is making the incandescent light bulb obsolete.

Modern cars are so smooth, quiet and reliable: no grease nipples to service every six months; no breaking axles; no noisy diffs and gearboxes; no breaking down in the rain with water on the electrics; no overheating; virtually no punctures on trips; mostly, no serious rust problems, air conditioning, and so much more.

They used to say, "Never buy the first of a new model, until they have got all the bugs out and bring out series 2!"

The downside of modern cars is all the electronics. If things go wrong, you can't fix it yourself. All modern cars have inbuilt GPS trackers. Every trip you make can be monitored and recorded.

Cell phones and GPS make communication and travel so much easier!

Fuzzy screen, small TV's are a thing of the past but again, every phone call, every website and every T.V. program watched, can be monitored.

The Internet has pros and cons. Information, on any subject, is readily available. The downside is the easy access to pornography and violence. It de-sensitises people to reality and leads to addictions that are hard to break.

So many video games now, are of a violent nature. The hero is always the one who shoots, hurts or kills the most people.

The most annoying thing for me is advertising. You can't get away from it! It clogs up the letterbox; pops up on every website; ruins a good T.V. movie; and makes me change the radio station, on a regular basis! Some really irritate me, to the point that I refuse to watch or listen to them, but others I can tolerate a bit more. I think, the most memorable ads, have a little ditty or song attached to them.

It's interesting that our knowledge of health and diseases should mean that things like; obesity, heart disease and type-two diabetes are a thing of the past. Instead however, they are on the increase, as people make poor choices.

We should always have a plan and prepare for a worst-case scenario. What if we lost all power, and all electronics? No vehicle or communication? What if the entire monetary system collapsed and our cards, or even our cash—was worthless?

It would be wise to become as self-sufficient as possible; generate our own power; grow our own food; and even catch our own water.

Twenty-four

Old Age

One of the senior men at the power board was a bit of a 'hard' man; on his wife, his family, and the workers under him. He happened to get Alzheimer's at a relatively young age. I went around to his house to do a small job and I told his wife, how sorry I was for him. She said, "Don't worry about him! He doesn't have a care in the world! He has gone back to childhood. As long as he's warm and has food and drink, he is quite happy. Feel sorry for those whose mind is still very alert and active, but their body has packed-up, so they can't do the things they want to."

Generally speaking, the body ages faster than the mind does. I certainly don't feel as old as I look! Every time you lose a tooth; some more hair, or what is left has gone grey; when the glasses need a stronger lens; you don't hear so well: it's all a sign of inevitable progress.

When you read the health magazines; there are very persuasive arguments to buy an awful lot of supplements to help to keep the mind and body stronger for longer. However, I think that the most important thing is that you accept yourself the way you are, and stick to a good diet and exercise.

Twenty-five

Where Am I?

When I look in a mirror
What do I see?
I see a face, some clothes,
Some hair, a nose,
But I don't see me.

Where am I?
I'm hidden inside.
I'm under that skin,
And behind those eyes.

You can't look at my love
Or my pleasure or pain,
You can't see my knowledge
Or wisdom I've gained.

Where Am I?

My compassion for others,
The things I believe,
And the Prayers I've made;
You can't see these.

These are the things,
That make the real me.
They have no shape or form,
Only God can see.

When my human life is over,
And they lay me in the ground,
I will have long since left that body,
The real 'me' is still around.

And in a future time,
By God's great design and pleasure,
I'll be a new creation,
And live with him forever!

Twenty-six

The Horticultural Group

The only plants I've ever had success growing, have been succulents. When I started going out with Ani, she told me that she had wisteria at her house. I stayed away for a week because I thought it might be contagious!

We went out to a horticultural group one time, and this bloke came up to me and asked how my frangipanis were doing this year. I gave him a bit of a blank look as the cogs went around in my head; *"Think, Kev, think!* What the heck is a frangipani? It must be some sort of plant, but I have no idea! I better bluff my way through this one!"

"The PH level of my soil was wrong, so I added some dissolved magnesium sulphate. That seemed to help!" I blurted out. This time it was him that gave me the blank look! I guessed that he would have thought that, I was either an eccentric genius, or a total nut case. There is probably a bit of truth in either opinion, so I thought I had handled that well!

Twenty-seven

Work Stories

I had one job out in the country to install one extra power point in an old wool shed on a farm. It seemed pretty basic, as the switchboard had only two fuses on it; one for the lights, and the other for plugs. There were only two power points in the shed; one over the work bench, and the other on a far wall.

I turned on the bench grinder and pulled the plug fuse. The grinder stopped, so I went further on and cut into the circuit where they wanted the extra plug. There was a big flash and bang, and I found a chunk had been taken out of my side cutters! I didn't get a shock because I was holding insulated handles.

It didn't make sense so I turned off the main switch, killing all the lights as well. After grabbing my torch, I went back and banged the end of the wire with the side of my side cutters, to make sure it was now dead. Another flash and bang!

Now, even more confused, I opened the switchboard to find that the wire went through the wall to another old switchboard located back-to-back and labelled, 'hot water only'. The hot water cylinder was long gone, but someone had poked the wire through the adjacent wall, and put a power point on it! The fuse had wire wrapped around it several times, so that it would never blow. I now have a proximity tester that beeps whenever I get close to a live wire, so I don't cut into it!

The worst wiring job I have seen was in a shed up the coast. A single, 1mm red wire was taken from a power point, to an adjacent triple-light switch. A 3-core, 1mm wire came out from the switch, with the red, black and green wires split to go to three different lights! A black, 1mm wire was connected into another power wire with a strip connector, and this was looped to the three lights to provide the neutral!

I had another job; to replace a batten holder, in a bedroom for an old lady. It seemed like a ten minute job, so I agreed to do it for $20, to help her out. As soon as I undid the screws, the wire sprung back into the celling space! After getting up into the man hole, I found that the wire was not only short, it was perished as well! Just over an hour later, I got the job finished. She got her money's worth!

Another time, I had a job to replace a broken power point for another little old lady. Again, it was a ten minute job that I was going to do cheap. There was an old china cabinet next to it that I needed to move about two feet. I lifted one end to see how heavy it was and to decide if I needed to empty it, but the front leg promptly fell off! I couldn't hold it with one hand and grab the leg with the other, so I had to put it down. The whole thing tilted forward, making the fine china inside fall against the glass.

"Ooh, you broke my cabinet!" the lady screamed, *"I hope you haven't broken the china as well!"* She didn't believe that I had discovered the cabinet was just sitting on the unattached leg; that someone had broken it previously. Emptying the cabinet took a long time, as I wasn't allowed to touch much of its contents, and she had to tell me the stories behind her collection.

I then had to clear out the back of my van enough to fit the cabinet and, after assuring her that my friend could fix it like new, (she wouldn't trust me) I took it home and drilled, screwed and glued it back to strength. After waiting long enough, so that the glue wasn't going to drip on her carpet, I returned it to the spot, next to the now, new power point to get everything reinstated.

Another job was at a security-conscious mansion. They told me how to lock the house, where to put the key after I had finished, and told me to snip the padlock on the large gates as I left. I followed the directions precisely, but then I realised that I had locked myself in, as the small exit gate was also securely locked!

The gates were un-climbable so I went back into the house and looked, unsuccessfully, for keys. I got into the back courtyard and realised that I could climb the back fence (just). I locked the house again; climbed a side gate to the courtyard, clambered over the back fence (hoping no one was watching) and walked around the corner to my van!

More recently, I had a very busy day, so I started work about 7am when it was just getting light. At about 9am I was ready to go to the next job, but found that I had left my lights on and the battery was flat! Fortunately, Gisborne is a small place and home was only about 20 minutes jog away. I jogged home, grabbed my jumper leads and drove back, in our Nissan Tiida. The van started o.k. with the jump start, so I locked the Tiida and drove the van home the long way, to charge the battery.

I then jogged back to pick up the Tiida, only to realise that the keys were in the van's glove box! After another jog home to get the keys, it was more of a fast walk back, to get the car again! Having driven the car back home to swap vehicles again, I was finally able to get to the next job! The dog didn't get a run that night!

I like it when I can bless people through my work; like the lady that was caring for my Dad at Beetham Village. She was a single mum with three kids and hadn't had any hot water at her home, for over two months. She asked me for a quote on the cost to fix it, so she could save up the money. I replaced her element at no cost as a way of thanking her, for the wonderful care she, and others, gave to my Dad in the last months of his life.

Another time, I was asked to evaluate a broken fridge and to write a letter for an insurance company, so the family could get another. I found the power point that the fridge was plugged into was faulty. She asked me if this had something to do with the kids getting electric shocks from the bedroom! An hour-and-a-half later, I had replaced several power points and repaired the switchboard. She had about $30 in her wallet, so I accepted that as full payment.

Part of the reason I am writing my books is because I would like to do electrical work for needy people; to bless them, rather than having to work and charge market rates, to make a living.

I enjoyed my 22 years working at the power board. We got to travel large distances through some of the most beautiful scenery in the country, and meet many interesting people and places.

I was a young apprentice when I first stayed at the Manutahi Hotel in Ruatoria. We had a few days work at the substation there. We went to the bar for a drink before tea, and this big 'Maori' bloke pointed at me. *"Come here boy!"* he shouted. I looked at my workmates; they just smiled and indicated for me to go. *"Come *here, I said!*" he repeated, and he took off his belt. I thought he was going to give me a hiding, but I guessed my mates would step in if he hurt me.

I walked up to him and he held his belt out. "Let's see if we can get this around you twice!" he laughed... and he did! Everyone burst out laughing and he slapped me on the back, just about knocking me over. "I better shout you a beer and fatten you up, you skinny little 'pakeha' bastard!" he said.

My first wife's family were from up the coast, so I was made an honorary Ngati Poru. Nearly everyone wanted to know your whakapapa, so I would mention a few names and it was: "Come and meet your cuzzies!" I would be shouted beers at the bar, and often have crayfish crawling around the back of the work truck after a coast trip! In return, we would often spend a few hours fixing 'coast' electrics at people's houses!

The power board brought out a policy that repairs to the electrical system on the consumer side of the pole were chargeable to the consumer; whereas, if a fault was on the network side, it was non-chargeable, even if it was caused by extreme weather events.

Attitude made a difference, as often in storm conditions staff would work long hours to get power restored. If we turned up at a house and the consumer got angry about how long the power had been off, we would make it chargeable, but if they offered us a hot drink or a feed from their gas cooker, we would make it non chargeable regardless of where the fault was.

Getting back to domestic, one lady asked me to repair the over bench light that had never worked in her kitchen. It was old, so I replaced it. She phoned to say it still wasn't working.

I went back the next day and checked everything but found

nothing was wrong. She phoned that night to say it still wasn't working, so I went around after tea, turned the switch on, and it worked.

"How did you do that?" she asked.

"I turned the switch on," I replied.

"What switch?"

"The wall switch by the light."

"Oh, I've never touched that switch," she exclaimed, *"I never knew what it did!"*

Health-and-safety compliance regulation and the paperwork involved in the electrical industry has gone way over the top, in proportion to the risks, just as it has in the building and other trades. The Electrical Regulations book has a large portion taken up with telling you what the fine is if you don't comply with whatever regulations. They charge you a silly amount of money to purchase it and they are constantly updating it, without letting the electricians know, other than at the biannual refresher courses.

In reality, when someone or something gets hurt or damaged, there is never just one reason. It is always a combination of events or conditions that, however unlikely, happen simultaneously. In practice, it is far easier for a competent electrician to get the basics of polarity, earthing and protection right than it is to get them wrong—without the sometimes unnecessary regulations and paperwork.

Skin rashes

When I worked in the Power Board Transformer Department, we were exposed to a lot of toxic oils and chemicals; including transformer oil, Toluene, kerosene, white spirits, paints and paint thinners. Epoxy resins were also used in cable jointing and when replacing broken insulators. I developed severe skin rashes while working with, and around, these products that did not clear up when I stopped working there.

One time, the doctors wanted to do the prick allergy test on me to determine what else I was allergic to, but they could not find enough clear skin on my body to carry out the test! They had to use the blood test method instead. The rashes were often very itchy and I constantly had blood on my clothing and bedding. I had some strange ways of dealing with it.

I would run a hot bath, using just the hot tap at the end of filling it. I would keep my hand in the water until it was too hot to keep it in any longer. I would then rake my body with my finger nails, as hard as I could, until I was bleeding all over. Finally, I would straddle myself over the bath and drop myself in. The feeling was very intense; both pleasure and pain at the same time. I would nearly faint, but if I stayed very still in the bath, it didn't seem to scold me. After a few minutes, the water would cool down enough for me to wash myself.

After getting out of the bath, I would still have mild pain, but the itch would be gone. This made it more pleasant and easier to sleep with. I would then rub myself with cortisone cream, vinegar or, I would often have a large bowl of ice that I would melt over my body. The last step was usually to wrap myself in bandages, like a mummy. The only medication that would clear the rashes was Prednisone, so I had relatively large doses, periodically, to keep it under control. It was interesting that when I went to Fiji for three weeks voluntary work based on the Mercy Ship, the rashes cleared up. They came back as soon as I got back home.

The doctors said that I was allergic to wheat, milk, eggs, dairy, animals and house dust, and that I was to avoid sea food like crayfish. I had been having six weetbix with milk for breakfast; I so changed to cornflakes or muesli with soy milk for a while, but it made no difference.

When Ani was going out with me, she wanted to help me to get it cleared up, as it was not very attractive! She cut from my diet; sugar, cow's milk, coffee and caffeine, and gave me Kawakawa juice to drink. It worked! I can have all of the bad things, in moderate amounts, but any excess causes my skin to flare up. I still get rashes; every time I have to work in houses that have Insul-fluff or Pink Batts, and when I'm working with some soils.

The Boss

Your employer, or whoever pays you money, carries a significant amount of control over your life. They determine your level of income; your standard of living; when you have holidays, and for how long. They strongly influence your health, fitness level and sense of wellbeing. Many people spend more time with workmates than anyone else.

Early in their life, a person should decide what they are good at; what their main interests and passions are. They should then work out some way to get someone to pay them to do what they enjoy doing the most.

Twenty-eight

Flies

The common household fly is surprisingly hard to kill. Next time you fly spray your house; sweep up all the dead flies, put them in a box or jar with an air supply, and see how many are alive again 12 hours later. It may surprise you!

I did an experiment once, and repeated it with the same result. I caught a live fly and drowned it in water. After it had been submerged for three days, I took the fly out and put it on a paper towel. I then got some salt and sprinkled it on the fly. Using a cotton bud, I brushed the salt off and kept repeating this, until the fly moved. Before long, it flew away!

If you want to swat a fly; attack it head-on, as a fly can't take off backwards!

Twenty-nine

Cups and Saucers

One day, when I was a single parent, we were invited out for tea at a couple's house. I was given a cup of tea in a nice tea cup, and my son commented, "Look! The cup and saucer match! They have the same pattern on them!"

"Yes," I said. "A cup and saucer go together, so they normally match."

"Oh," he replied, "I thought it was called a saucer, because that is what you put tomato sauce on!"

I realised then that, my children had missed out, on some of the finer etiquettes in life! Perhaps I should have made them eat all the greens on their plates and the sandwich crusts, as well!

Thirty

The Root of all Evil

They say that money is the root of all evil, but it is not. Pride is!

Look at traffic offences: speeding, dangerous driving, drunk driving; all committed with the attitude, "I am a good driver, I can handle it safely".

Violence and abuse: "How dare you talk to me like that?"

Murder: "My life is more important than your life!"

Sexual abuse: "I will do it, because it gives me pleasure!"

Stealing: "I deserve nice things too, and I want it!"

Drug abuse: "I want the best high that I can get!"

Colonisation: "We know what's best for you!"

War, either: "We want what you have got!" or: "We are right and you are wrong!"

It's hard to think of a crime that does not involve pride. There are exceptions to all of this, as some people have had to steal to survive, or have committed a crime out of loyalty to, or protection for, others.

Interestingly, the further up the education, wealth, status, or power ladder you go; the more likely you are to be unfaithful to your partner and abuse or manipulate others. This is because you are in a position of power and control, and are therefore, less likely to be held accountable.

This is shown, in the number of celebrities and politicians that have 'fallen from grace'; who have had to explain their actions, once the word has got out.

We also need to be aware of the 'honey trap'! There are beautiful young girls out there who know what they have, and how to use it to their own advantage; often for money, blackmail, influence or fame. Often they themselves, are victims; used against their will, under coercion by others.

Thirty-one

Hatred and Unforgiveness

If there is someone that, you will walk on the other side of the road to avoid, or thoughts of them bring feelings of hatred or anger; then you are letting that person that you dislike so much have some control over your life. For your own well-being, you need to break free from that. This normally involves forgiving them for some wrong they have done against you.

This does not mean that you are letting them off the hook, or that what they did was not wrong or serious. You can forgive a person and still follow through with having them charged for a criminal conviction, if this is applicable. Forgiveness is not for the other person's benefit. It is essential, for your own personal well-being. Without diminishing the seriousness of anything that may have happened in the past, you must decide to move on; otherwise you will be locked into a perpetual victim mode.

Forgiveness is not dependent on the response, or the attitude of the person that you are going to forgive. In some cases, that person may be diseased, not contactable, or they may not even have admitted that they have done anything wrong. If it is at all possible or feasible, telling that person that you forgive them could be very beneficial for both of you.

Regardless of their attitude, you must decide that they will no longer have any control over your life. The other person may have no idea if, or when, you have feelings of hatred toward them—so this is only making *you* feel bad, not *them*. Try to see things from the other person's perspective. Often, they have suffered trauma in their own lives, or they may have a total misunderstanding of what occurred. In most cases, they have unresolved issues that are affecting their attitude and actions.

Don't use forgiveness as a reason for not taking action, and/or putting things right, if this is required. An example of this would be a partner in an abusive relationship. They may repeatedly say that they forgive their partner, believing that things will change, when they really need to get out and possibly lay charges. Try to make sure that you, and everyone else are safe; wherever possible, try to put right anything that is wrong, and then forgive.

Thirty-two

Sorry?

We see it so often; with celebrities or politicians caught out by things they have said and are then, forced to apologise.

"If I have offended anyone, I am truly sorry!" they will say.

The apology is fake! A true apology cannot start with the word IF.

Criminals that are caught, will often say sorry to show remorse and/or, to get a lighter sentence. Their remorse is probably genuine, but not on behalf of the victim. They are sorry that they were caught and/or, for the shame and embarrassment they have brought upon themselves and their family. It can be hard to discern if there is any genuine remorse for any innocent victims of their crimes.

When a child is growing up, we teach them to 'say sorry' when they have done something wrong. If they say a quick and flippant, 'sorry', we might reprimand them and then tell them, to say it properly. If they drag out a slow 'sor-r-ry' with a sad face, we usually accept it as genuine. It can become little more than a polite thing to say; like saying "pardon me" after a burp. However, it can also become a tool that others can use to fool and manipulate people.

Thirty-three

The Justice System

True justice would be served when a perpetrator pays the full cost and/or takes all the pain, trauma and hurt away from the victim onto themselves; so that the victim could then carry on with their lives, as if the crime never occurred. We all know that this cannot happen. It would also involve ensuring that the crime is never repeated in the future. That is quite achievable in many cases, but sadly, little investment is made to do this. So many times we read in the paper about repeat drink-drivers, for example; often their third or fourth time.

Putting a number in a circle at the roadside is not going to slow a speeding driver. Putting up a 'KEEP OFF THE GRASS' sign is not going to keep anyone off the grass, unless they choose to obey. A violent drunkard about to hurt somebody, is not going to stop and consider a fine, or the consequences of their actions. Legislation is always being tweaked to make the punishment fit the crime, but this does little in prevention.

I would propose a radical, new approach. First time offenders, for most crimes, would get little or no punishment other than counselling and education to make them aware of the consequences of their actions. Other factors; such as drug and alcohol abuse, or domestic violence, could be identified and dealt with at the same time. Even a fairly minor crime, like theft, can have serious long term consequences for a victim.

Education programmes in all schools teaching basic life skills, such as; love, respect and empathy for others; how to deal with hurts and emotions; what to do with feelings of anger or rejection, etc; should be compulsory for all students. Many children do not experience normal, acceptable behaviour in their homes; so they don't know what an 'acceptable' standard is.

It is perfectly legal to waste hundreds of dollars on gambling; spend most of your time drunk; waste hours of time watching pornography on the computer; overdose on legal highs or prescription drugs; cover your body with horrible tattoos; listen to loud rock music all day; yell at the kids; live in a filthy home; not shower or bathe; have unprotected sex with multiple partners; use heaps of profanity and swear words; get grossly overweight; have fatty takeaways for most meals; drink nothing but alcohol and fizzy drinks—but is it good for you?

I know that Presbyterian Support Services run sessions, called 'Growing Through Grief', under their 'Seasons' programme. This should be funded and introduced into all classrooms for a start, perhaps with a little modification.

Sexual abuse is one of the worst crimes, as the consequences are more than just physical and last for many years, if not a lifetime. Somehow, victims are more likely to become perpetrators themselves, or attract further abuse.

I was taught the rhyme; "Sticks and stones may break my bones but names can never hurt me." This is so wrong! Physical scars will usually heal, but emotional scars are generally unseen and often not dealt with. A person's spoken word can literally bring either a blessing or a curse on another person. This is also true of self-spoken words and attitudes. A person that says, "I am always sick!" or "I am always tired!" or "I am always broke!" usually will be, until they have a conscious attitude change. There are good campaigns out there like; "It's not o.k.!" that need serious funding and expansion.

Isn't it crazy that sports' people; like a golfer, can get paid millions of dollars for knocking a ball into a hole with less shots than other golfers, while people that make a real difference in people's lives, and even save lives like; lifeguards, firemen, ambulance medics and counsellors, are often unpaid volunteers? Likewise, there are those that are paid; e.g. caregivers, but are often on very low wages.

Thirty-four

The Welfare System

I am very grateful for the New Zealand Welfare System, as it has supported me for over ten years, but it has its downsides. When I was left to bring up three children on my own in 1999, I had a six-week stand down period before I could receive any money. I had little savings, so during much of this period I was using my credit card to pay for everything.

Eastland Network, and others, offered me short-term contract work, but anything that I earned over $180 per week, had an 'abatement' of 70 cents in the dollar. On top of this, I was paying secondary tax and ACC levies, so I lost over 90% of what I earned! I only had to buy a pie for lunch and some petrol, to be worse off working, than I would have been by not working.

I had begged them to at least let me pay off my debt, but was told that they had no discretion over that. I had to stop earning over the $180; so consequently, I never got out of debt. They do not allow for things like Christmas, birthdays, or having to visit sick parents in another town. Even things like school books and uniforms, were regarded as things that I could have foreseen and therefore, should have budgeted for.

I asked them for a loan one time to buy something important, but they declined it because my expenses exceeded my income and therefore, I would have no means of paying it back. I said, "Great! Could you please increase my income, so that I could at least break even?" They got out the calculator, told me that it was a different formula this time, and showed me that I had about $30 a week to spare!

During my time as a single parent, I did voluntary work for: Awapuni Pre-School, Awapuni School, Presbyterian Support, Anglican Care, Random Acts of Kindness, childcare (officially and unofficially), Creative Space, and anywhere else I could help. My contribution to society was probably greater, than if I had been working and paying taxes.

This highlights a problem. The rules have to cover a range of people with very different backgrounds and needs. There are many who are on a benefit, through no fault of their own, and are actively helping in society like coaching school sports' groups, or visiting older people.

There are others, who will choose to have a baby as a career choice, or will, deliberately make themselves unemployable; through drug and alcohol addictions, or just a serious attitude problem. I've seen tenants destroy their rented property and then demand, that the government find them somewhere else to live!

Social workers need to have more flexibility to be able to help those that really need it. Rents should always be paid direct to the landlords and, preferably, the power too. Every contract for every beneficiary should include a clause; advising them of six-monthly home visits. This could not be considered an invasion of privacy, as it would be no different, from a landlord doing a property inspection. Those that can prove that they are actively involved in positive voluntary work should be exempt from any paid-work requirements.

Every classroom in every school needs one other person in the room at all times, to assist. This should be encouraged and supported; obviously, with the right people.

I know of two recent cases of employers; one in horticulture and one in forestry that were desperate for good workers. Both found the perfect workers among migrants on temporary work visas. They were offered and accepted fulltime positions, conditional on immigration letting them stay. Despite testimonials and pleas from the employers, the positions had to be offered to New Zealand citizens only.

Thirty-five

Christmas

When I was a single parent struggling on a small budget, Christmas came around. I decided that I was no longer going to buy anybody any Christmas presents. At the time, I had two local grandchildren, so I gave each of them a 'Papa' day. They had a day and night of my full attention, to do fun things together. After Christmas was over, they remembered their special day, more than the presents they received.

That was many years ago, and I haven't bought any Christmas presents since. Christmas, along with Easter, is a pagan festival that has been hijacked by Christians. Jesus was not born on 25th December and there is nothing in the Bible that indicates that we should celebrate His birth. A lot of people get confused between Jesus and Santa. Even songs give Santa, God-like qualities:

"He knows when you are sleeping, he knows when you're awake, he knows when you are bad or good, so be good, for goodness sake!"

Some people even liken prayer, to giving Santa a wish-list: "If you are good enough, your wish might come true!"

Easter is very messed up. The story of Jesus' death and resurrection is the most beautiful love story ever told. The Creator God loves His rebellious creation so much that, He sends His only Son, to be tortured and to die for our sins. This was so that, reconciliation could take place, and that ultimately we could spend eternity in Paradise, as originally intended. He rose from the grave, visited His friends for a few weeks, and then headed back to Heaven, to prepare a place for us.

There is little connection between bunny rabbits that lay chocolate eggs, and the death and resurrection of Jesus. Secular schools and pre-schools are not even allowed to teach the 'Christian' version. We shouldn't get too upset about this, as the correct biblical way to remember and celebrate, is via the 'breaking of bread' or 'communion'. Non-Christians are explicitly excluded.

Apart from all this, there is nothing wrong with enjoying and celebrating Christmas and Easter, however you want to do it. It is a good time for people, to hear and learn about these Christian stories, when and where possible.

Thirty-six

The Gift

Every day, each one of us is given a gift. We all get the same gift. We can waste and squander it away, or we can use it wisely. That gift is 'time'. That is why it is called 'the present'. We all get the same amount, but it travels at a different speed for each of us. For some, the day drags on and they can't wait for it to end. For others, it goes too quick and they don't get the things done that they wanted to do.

The most valuable thing that you can do with time is to share it with others. Older people, and young children especially, just love someone to sit down and spend time with them. Most of the time, you don't have to plan or do anything. Just being there and perhaps, talking, will often be the highlight of someone's day.

Use your time wisely; it is a valuable asset and you don't know when yours is going to run out!

Thirty-seven

Time Travel

Time is affected by mass, acceleration and gravity. Time travel is not only theoretically possible, it actually occurs, in practice. Clocks in satellites and space stations are set to run slower than those on Earth.

If two people synchronised their watches and flew at supersonic speed around the earth; one going east and one going west, and arrived back at the same destination, their watches would be out of synch with each other by a small but measurable amount when they got back to their starting point.

If matter accelerated close to the speed of light, the Lorentz factor would kick in. The distance to travel to get to a destination actually decreases, so that the arrival time is quicker than expected.

Time is sometimes a matter of perspective. If someone is watching a parade at ground level, it might take 20 minutes for the parade to pass by. If another person was watching the same parade from a high roof top, they would be able to see the start and finish at one glance, taking the time factor out of the event.

It's interesting to talk to people who have been in cars that have rolled down a bank. They will describe how everything seemed to go in slow motion, and that it seemed to go on forever. Then you will hear the comment that, "My life flashed before my eyes!" It's like they go into a time warp, not knowing whether, they are going to live or die. Trauma distorts time.

Turn Back Time

> If I could fly faster than the speed of light,
> And travel around the sun,
> I would arrive back home in the blink of an eye,
> Before I had begun.
> Then watch myself on my frantic flight,
> Like an All Black try re-run!

Thirty-eight

The Meaning of Life
(and other words of wisdom)

The most important things in life are love and relationships. We need to get our relationships right with God, family and those around us.

When an older person is sitting alone in their house without anyone calling or caring; it doesn't matter whether they are sitting in luxury or poverty, or what they have done in life. They will be sad. Solitary confinement is regarded as a cruel punishment. You don't always have to have answers in order to help somebody in need. Often, just listening and showing that you care is enough to make a difference.

When a child does something wrong, speak against the action, not the person. For example; instead of, "You must be stupid to do something like that," you could say, "You are a clever kid, so why did you choose to do such a stupid thing?"

If someone has a problem that you need to speak to them about, a way to do it effectively is to put the problem on yourself. For example; instead of, "You have a drinking problem and it makes you nasty. You need to sort yourself out!," try, "I have a problem with your drinking; your change in attitude scares me. What can we do about it?"

We were given two ears and one mouth for a reason. There are awards for good speaking, but there are none for good listening. A wise man speaks because he has something to say. A foolish man speaks because he has to say something. Learn to be a good listener. The only thing worse than a man who doesn't know, is a man who doesn't know that he doesn't know.

Our lives are like the ripples of a stone thrown into a pond. Everything that we say or do affects those around us, and those who are closest are affected the most. May our ripples be good ones! Live your life in such a way that the world would be a better place for having you in it!

'Like' will always look after 'like'. The poor look after the poor, and the rich look after the rich. A person may say that they wish they were wealthy so that they could give generously and help others. Others give generously from what they have, and get blessed for it.

Don't make plans, plans change. Have dreams, a dream can last forever.

Thirty-nine

The God Connection

Evolution

First, there was nothing. Out of nothing, came every bit of matter in the universe. All of this matter somehow came together in a big ball that suddenly exploded, and everything flew apart at huge speed! As it was separating, some matter started joining together and over millions of years, matter separated into solid, liquid and gas. In perfect proportions for life, things started being made that were more complex than a modern day computer!

Not only did life randomly appear, but two of everything happened to evolve, with reproductive organs so they could start reproducing themselves. Out of the same dirt, beautiful plants and fruit trees just happened to invent themselves. A whole balanced ecosystem just happened to evolve at the same time.

Just look at the lifecycle of a butterfly or a frog; look at animals and fish that change colour; glow worms and fireflies. Take time to smell the flowers; taste a variety of foods, and then tell me that everything was just 'random chance'. I don't think so!

A caterpillar turning into a butterfly is the equivalent of a car building its own garage, transforming into an aeroplane and flying away! There is no doubt that things change and adapt. If you put an insect with eyes in complete darkness for generations, that species will probably lose the ability to see well. On the other hand if you put a blind creature in daylight for generations, I doubt that it will grow eyes, no matter how many thousands of years you leave it!

Nearly all creatures were larger, millions of years ago; mammals, birds and fish. So rather than things starting off small and basic, and then growing larger and more complex over millions of years; all the evidence points to much larger creatures getting smaller. A human has always been a human and an ape has always been an ape.

At school we were being taught the evolution theory, and the subject of the missing link came up, in regards to the transition from ape to human. My school mates would point to me and say, "Here he is; the 'Missen' link!"

Foot in both camps

I was brought up in a rather strict church and family. Sundays were spent in 'Sunday best' clothes that included shirt and tie for me, from a fairly young age. Sunday school was first, followed by church services, morning and evening. I sat through some rather long and boring sermons on hard pews. I always swore that when I had children of my own, I would never subject them to that.

We didn't own a car but Dad used to borrow a near-new Mark One Cortina, to do a Sunday school pickup. My sister and I still had to walk for half an hour to church on most Sunday mornings, to save Dad another trip. Grandma used to come over for lunch quite often, as Dad had the use of the car to pick her up. After lunch she would have an afternoon nap and we all had to be quiet.

The highlight of our Sundays was the Sunday drive after we dropped Grandma off. We would often drive around the new housing development areas and look at the new houses being built.

In our church, we weren't allowed to take part in communion unless we had been baptised. When I was about 13-years-old, I asked to be baptised. I felt like I had taken another step towards manhood after taking part in communion. When I was asked to speak or take part in church services, I would get compliments and encouragement that was lacking in other areas of my life.

After moving to Gisborne, I helped to run a Sunday school; a job I was good at and enjoyed. I bought my first van, a rusty old Thames Freighter; put a couple of old couches in the back and used it to pick up the Sunday school kids.

On the outside, I looked like the perfect Christian boy. On the inside, I was confused. A sad old man would preach that: "The Joy of the Lord is our strength; the pleasures of this world are only fleeting and don't bring true happiness; the life of a wicked man leads to destruction!"

Those that were not involved in church seemed very happy and they didn't seem to be self-destructing. I decided to have a foot in both camps, so my lifestyle outside church was quite different to the one I showed inside.

Things came to an inevitable head when the church heard about my alternative lifestyle and I was publicly disciplined by the church. I had to leave home for a while because I was showing no repentance. I knew that I had done wrong in the church's eyes, but the attitude, of some of the church members did not seem right. I decided to look for the truth.

I found one of the few positive references to religion in James 1:27. "True religion is this; to visit the widows and orphans in their affliction and to keep oneself unspotted from the world."

I knew I had blown the last part, so I decided to visit the most helpless widow I knew. She was an old lady crippled with arthritis, by the name of Doris Brooking. She knew what I had done, as she was part of the church and I didn't know what I was going to say to her, but I went to visit anyway. She gave me a big smile and invited me in, put the kettle on and gave me tea and biscuits.

I didn't have to say anything. She told me that she had been praying for me every day and shared some very interesting tales; about the mischief that she had got up to in her youth and, how 'real' God was to her now. I had gone to somehow help or cheer her up, but it was I that got the blessing! Women were not allowed to take part in regular church services, but I found her to be the nicest, wisest, most godly person I knew!

What had appeared to be a disaster in my life, turned out to be a good thing. I had previously been very judgemental of other people and was full of pride. My life was a bit of a mess, but God answered my cry for help. I tried changing some of my ways, but kept failing and feeling guilty. One day I cried out to God, "I give up! You made me this way. If You have a problem with my desires, then You fix it!" He did!

The guilt and struggle disappeared and slowly, unhealthy desires disappeared also. I learned a very important lesson. You can't try to be a good Christian. God's standard is too high for anyone to keep. When you invite Jesus into your life, God sends His Spirit, to join with your spirit, so that your desires become His desires. That's why God answers prayers; because you are asking Him for things that He wants to have happen anyway. He will transform your mind and help you to be the person that you should be. It should not be a constant struggle to try and do the right thing.

Dealing with adult issues

My 'God connection' grew and my understanding of how things should be; but it was in my later years that I had my worst issues. I did some terrible things that hurt a lot of people. In fact, it was the people, whom I loved the most that I hurt the most. Why? I spent many hours with counsellors, praying and self-analysing; asking that very question. I could even say that I've spent years on it, as it often pops up in my mind.

Obviously, regardless of my good intentions, I had issues in my life that I had not dealt with. As with all things that go wrong in this world, there is never just one reason; it is always a combination of contributing factors. Satan, the devil, Lucifer, whatever you want to call him; him and his demons are a beaten foe. They hate God so much that they are going to drag, as many people down with them as possible so that they won't receive God's love, forgiveness and salvation.

They will focus their attack, especially on his representatives here on earth, the Christians, because they are his biggest threat. They have even infiltrated organised religion to do so. One thing that God will never do for anybody is to make their decisions for them. Satan also, is unable to make you do anything. You always have to take responsibility for your own actions. What he does do, is blind you to the truth, so that you may be unaware that you are so far off track. That is where reading and following the Bible, prayer, and having Christian friends helps. I am thankful that God never stops loving us; will always forgive us when we are repentant; that we can never mess things up so bad that He can't turn a disaster into something good. Some will say that once a person becomes a Christian, demons cannot remain in them. I know that they had a strong influence over my life for many years. We read a lot about Jesus and His disciples casting out demons in the Bible, but we don't see it much in today's western society. They are alive, well and active.

Satan offers a carrot in front of your nose and then whacks you with a stick from behind. The devil does not look after his own. This is most clearly seen in rock stars. They sell their soul to the devil for fame and fortune, but few of them find happiness and many die young. Demons' greatest control over people is through sex, pornography, drugs, alcohol and music.

It's interesting that many of the greatest songs ever written talk of spiritual things:

Led Zeppelin's *Stairway to Heaven*
"Yes, there are two paths you can go by but in the long run
There's still time to change the road you're on."

Queen's *Bohemian Rhapsody*
"Beelzebub has a devil put aside for me…
Nothing really matters, anyone can see
Nothing really matters, nothing really matters to me
Any way the wind blows"

John Lennon's *Imagine*

> "Imagine there's no heaven
> It's easy if you try
> No hell below us
> Above us only sky
> Imagine all the people living for today"

What a disaster that would be! Every man for himself!

The Eagles' *Hotel California*

Perhaps we should take note of the description of being stuck in hell...

> "And I was thinking to myself
> 'This could be heaven or this could be hell'
> And she said, 'we are all just prisoners here,
> of our own device'
> Last thing I remember, I was
> Running for the door
> I had to find the passage back to the place I was before
> 'Relax' said the night man
> 'We are programmed to receive
> You can check out any time you like,
> But you can never leave!'"

These are just a few examples of many popular songs that I have used to help you to be aware of the messages that the lyrics are sending to your brain. Some are subliminal, some are blatant. Backward masking is also often present, intended or not. I'm not saying that you shouldn't listen to the songs, but be aware that they can influence your thinking.

Hollywood

It's no coincidence that 'holly' wood is used by witches and wizards in their witchcraft. Many actors call upon the spirit world to possess them, so that they 'become' the characters they represent. Movies are used to determine much of the world's moral standards and to 'normalise' abnormal behaviour.

When the masses are entertained, they don't think for themselves. This is another form of mass people-control.

There are so many religions and churches all claiming to be right. So how do I know which is the right one?

No religion is going to save you! Religion is man seeking GOD. True Christianity is GOD reaching down to mankind and saying, "I love you just the way you are. Jesus died on the cross for your sins; ask Him into your life and let Him be there for you."

Most of the mainline churches are pretty much on track. It isn't so bad that there are so many different churches, as long as they stick to the basic truths and work with each other. There are so many different types of people; some like big churches with loud music and some prefer a quieter, family-like atmosphere.

There are also a lot of different issues that churches have different interpretations on, like the day of worship—original Sabbath (Saturday) or Sunday; speaking in tongues; spiritual healings. Do we go straight to Heaven (or Hell) when we die, or do we remain asleep until Judgment Day? Is Hell eternal punishment or are the consequences of judgement eternal (death)? Are Christians raptured before, during, or after the time of tribulation? Who, or what is the Antichrist, and the mark of the beast; and can a Christian lose his salvation? And many more controversial subjects that will always be debated, but aren't hugely important in the big picture.

Be wary of 'progressive Christianity' that says that all religions and beliefs lead to God and that we all just have to love each other. This is very wrong.

If God is a God of love, how come there is so much suffering in this world?

As mentioned earlier, we all have free will to make our own decisions. Those decisions will have consequences and no one is exempt from them. GOD never promised anyone an exemption from trouble, but He did promise to be there to help you through, if you ask Him.

Atheists say that they don't believe in God, but if you ask them to describe the God they don't believe in, they would usually describe a cruel, unjust God that I don't believe in either!

The Bible is a collection of 66 books; 39 of them in the Old Testament that was written before Jesus was born. The amazing thing is that His birth, life, death and resurrection were predicted with 100 percent accuracy in the Old Testament, hundreds of years before these events occurred! The odds of this happening are astronomical!

Every prophecy in the Bible has either come true, or is just about to. Noah's Ark has been found; the remains of Egyptian chariots have been found, from the crossing of the Israelites through the

Red Sea; and the Ark of the Covenant has been found; all proving that the Biblical stories are true.

You can't make or measure cold. Cold is just the absence of heat. You can't make or measure darkness; it is just the absence of light. In the same way, the more of God we take out of this world, the closer to Hell it becomes. When I use the term God, I mean the Biblical Creator God; Jehovah, Yahweh; who sent His Son Jesus to Earth, and the Holy Spirit. Many terrible things have been done, and are being done, in the name of God. He is 'Love' and if anybody is showing hatred towards their fellow man, then they are following the God of this world, Satan; not the true God.

'Act of God' is a legal term to describe unforeseen natural disasters. Many will see innocent people suffer and use these events and things like massacres, child deformities and sicknesses, etc; as a reason to deny the existence of a loving God. They deny His ability to control the world, or portray Him as a hateful tyrant, with little love at all!

Look at it from the other side. Do all parents that have a healthy child give God the credit, and thank Him? Do people thank God every day, for their life, the sunshine, the good things? Most people don't. If we lived in a perfect world with no war, sickness, disease, hunger, etc; people would say, "What do I need God for? Life is fine without Him!"

It's in times of trouble that we call out to God for help. It's in these times that we see answered prayer and experience His love and comfort. That's how our faith is strengthened, and it's how we know He is real.

God created man in His own image, because He wanted to share good things. He didn't want robots; He gave us free will so that we could love Him back. He wants nothing but the best for us.

The rain falls on the just and the unjust alike, or, as a great philosopher once put it, shit happens! We are sinful people living in a sinful world. God does not exempt us from the consequences of our own actions. If we choose to live an unhealthy lifestyle, we are more prone to sickness and disease. If we pollute the environment and clear-fell vast areas of forest, we are more prone to natural disasters. If we expose people to copious amounts of violence on T.V., in movies and games or even in real life; we are more likely to have it acted out.

God never promised anyone at any time, a life free of stress or trauma, but what He does promise is that, if we ask Him, He will be there to help us through.

We know, through Biblical prophecy, that this world is doomed. There will be a huge increase in natural disasters, floods, earthquakes, fires, famine and wars. There will be a one-world government and one-world religion. They will have control over all trading, possibly through microchipping. Hatred towards Jews and Christians will increase. The Biblical standards of right and wrong are even now regarded as unacceptable, as they are seen to discriminate against those that choose alternative lifestyles.

God will honour those that stay faithful to Him and His principles, and we will see even greater miracles and healings, etc.

Forty

A brief description of what I believe

God always was. He is outside the restrictions of time, space and matter. He created heaven and heavenly creatures first. Satan was God's right hand man, but due to pride, he rebelled against God and wanted His position. He was banished from heaven, along with one third of the angels. God did not just kill him, because the other creatures would have then obeyed, because of fear, not love. Satan's true colours had to be revealed so that God could be seen as just.

God created the earth and mankind, so that He could have a relationship with them. Again, He had to offer free choice and again, His creatures rebelled. Paradise was lost, but God's love was so great that He still wanted us to experience His ultimate goodness.

Jesus was always part of God. He willingly gave up His heavenly position to come to earth as a baby; suffer terribly, feeling all human pain and emotion—ultimately to face torture and crucifixion on a Roman cross.

He died so that the requirements of justice and mercy were fulfilled. Any punishment that we deserve for our sin was paid for, by Him on the cross. Jesus rose again and returned to the right hand of God.

Not long after He left, God sent His Holy Spirit to dwell within Christians. His Spirit opens our eyes to another dimension. We are able to see God working, to understand Him, and to have direct communication with God Himself, through prayer.

I believe that when we die, we cease to exist. We don't have a separate soul that instantly goes to Heaven or Hell. One day, Jesus is going to return and the dead will rise first to meet Him in the air and those Christians living, will also be raised up and taken to Heaven.

On earth, the Antichrist will demand that all people have his mark on their forehead or right hand (possibly a microchip), and worship him, or they will be killed. This is likely to be the start of the seven-year tribulation period.

There will be powerful witnesses for Christ that have His protection, but the cost of choosing Him over the Antichrist will be high. After the time of tribulation, Jesus will return again with His 'bride', the raptured Christians, and defeat the Antichrist, the Beast, and their followers.

This will be the start of the 'Millennium', a thousand years of peace, in which the entire earth will be ruled by Christ, His bride and the martyrs. After the thousand years, Satan will be loosed from his chains for a short time, gather an army from all over the earth and surround Jerusalem again. God will send fire down from heaven to devour them. The devil will finally be cast into the lake of fire where the Beast and the Antichrist are. All the dead will be resurrected, and together with the living, will be judged.

Those who have accepted Jesus Christ into their lives will spend eternity with Him in the new paradise. They will receive rewards depending on their works and lifestyle.

Those who choose not to accept Jesus will be punished. I don't believe this will be eternal suffering in Hell, but I believe punishment will equate to a person's actions. Ultimately, the effects will be eternal, as the person will cease to exist.

The Meal Prayer

Thank you, Lord, for Friends and Family and Fellowship and Fun, and for this Feast of Fine Food Found before us to Feed and Fortify our Feeble Frames. To our Faithful Father in Heaven, we are Forever grateful. Amen!

Forty-one

What Next?

I've wanted to write this book for many years, and have enjoyed every minute of it! I would like to make a recording of my original songs, and/or make a movie or two!

I have two movie ideas. One is about a man that is suicidal, but decides that rather than die sad; he is going to seek all the pleasures this world has to offer, regardless of the consequences, before taking his own life. What he does and doesn't find pleasurable, surprise him! Maybe it will be my next book before the movie!

The other idea would be to make a movie based on the book of Revelation. This would be far more adventurous and difficult, as it would involve huge beasts and creatures, large battles, and mass destruction. The heavenly scenes would have thousands of angels and God Himself!

Many people have a story to tell. I would encourage anyone to tell it. Don't worry about how good it is, or who will read it; just make a start and let it flow! You might surprise yourself and others!

The Word Trip

A picture paints a thousand words,
Or so the story goes.
But a picture is just a static thing,
It can't change or grow!

I will use but simple words,
That well up from the heart,
To paint a picture in your mind,
As clear as any art.

As the story goes on, the picture changes,
Like a movie on a screen.
Your imagination takes you places
That you have never been.

With the story ended and the last words read,
This book is put away,
But your heart's desire is a crave for more,
Another trip, another day!

The End!

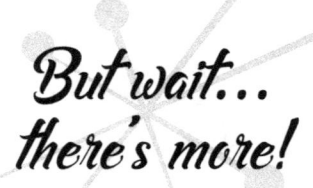

But wait... there's more!

Other Books by Kevin Missen

Random Streams of Poetic Dreams
illustrated by Dale Wilkie
My largest compilation of poetry.

Messages from the Other Side
Funeral poems covering Christian and secular.

Two Sides to a Wounded Heart
A love story about a couple that split up and then got back together again.

The locomotive that stayed alive: The story of WA165
A poetic history of Gisborne's iconic steam engine.

Hamish's Horror Holiday
The story of a boy that spent days lost in the bush.

Current contacts
    www.kevani.co.nz
    Missen Publishing
    Email: missen.k@xtra.co.nz

www.ingramcontent.com/pod-product-compliance
Lightning Source LLC
Chambersburg PA
CBHW071405290426
44108CB00014B/1692